IGNATIUS

C. Dalton Jones

18 · August 2006.

Ignatius St Lawrence SJ

IGNATIUS

Founder of the Jesuits

 St Paul Publications

Cum permissu Superiorum
25th April 1990

St Paul Publications
Middlegreen, Slough SL3 6BT, United Kingdom

ISBN 085439 337 4

Printed by The Guernsey Press Co., Guernsey C.I.

St Paul Publications is an activity of the priests and brothers of the Society of St Paul who proclaim the Gospel through the media of social communication

Contents

Foreword

St Ignatius was a man with big ideas and great courage. His story should be read by anyone who wants to know what a true hero is like. I say "true" because St Ignatius started off with a wrong idea of a hero. It took a cannon ball and much patient teaching by God to show him how true heroes behave.

Father St Lawrence, whose name is also Ignatius, tells his story in sixteen short and very readable chapters. Though the world we live in has changed a lot since the time of Ignatius, there is still much we can learn from his life. More than ever today we need his clear understanding of how to be led by God, his untiring pursuit of all that is good and right, his way of winning over others, his enthusiasm, his bravery. He talked much about God's greater honour and service. This book shows how he lived what he preached. It can also give us ideas of how to do the same.

Later this year, on September 27th, we celebrate the 450th anniversary of the founding of the Jesuits. And next year, it is the 500th anniversary of St Ignatius' birth. No one could ever count the thousands and thousands of young people who have been educated by Jesuits all over the world since they began. A recent book on Jesuit education speaks of one and half million pupils and students in Jesuit schools and universities today in 56 countries. It is important they know something about the man who started it all. This book, written especially for them, explains what sort of person he was and the ideas that he had. I strongly recommend it to all young people to be read during these coming anniversary months.

Michael Campbell-Johnston SJ
April 1990

Introduction

My interest in St Ignatius of Loyola goes back as far as I can remember, having received his name in Baptism. After frequently preaching on him in my days as a schoolmaster, I gradually realised that I had rarely got beyond the drama of his wound in battle and the fresh start he made through reading the lives of Christ and the saints. Hence, when I had finished with teaching, I decided to spend my time in putting into a book the whole story of Ignatius, telling it with younger readers in mind, but at the same time so choosing my words that the book would also be readable by those adults who wanted a brief and simple outline of the lives of Ignatius and the early Jesuits.

The story is naturally based on some of the modern lives of Ignatius. I have been able to add local colour as a result of visiting a number of the places which he himself visited or in which he lived. Various friends in various age-groups have kindly read the manuscript. Further, I have tried it out on some of the young people of the age I have in mind, even to the extent of being asked to reserve copies for them.

Being neither a trained student of History nor an expert in English composition, I have relied on others to advise and criticise about the text. Amongst these I single out for thanks my fellow-Jesuits Philip Caraman and David Hoy, as also

Richard Milward Esq and my brother Raleigh.

Another to whom I am most grateful is Fr Ignacio Zavalla SJ who was so generous with his time when I was in Loyola, guiding me round and explaining many details not to be found in books.

I dedicate the book to the boys of Donhead School, Wimbledon, who unknowingly inspired me to write it, and also to those of St John's, Beaumont, who, again unknowingly, encouraged me to complete it. I shall indeed be happy if what I have written about one saint, Ignatius of Loyola, born in 1491, should inspire some of our generation, five hundred years later, as those "holy books" inspired Ignatius himself to devote his life A.M.D.G.

Ignatius St Lawrence
May 1990

Readers will find at the end of certain chapters some Notes. These have been added so as to give fuller details about places or people whose names have occured, e.g. what Loyola is like today; the journeys of Francis Xavier; the first Jesuit school in England.

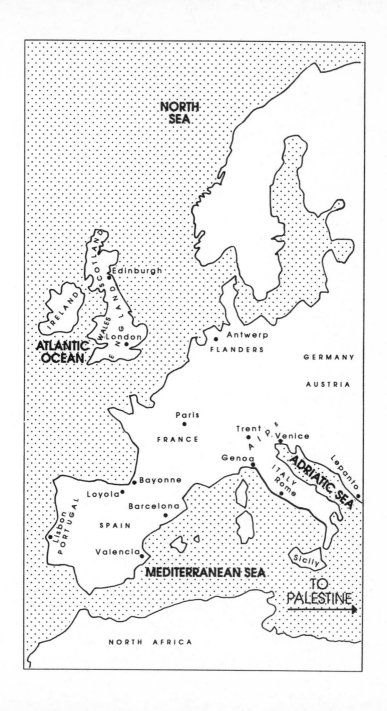

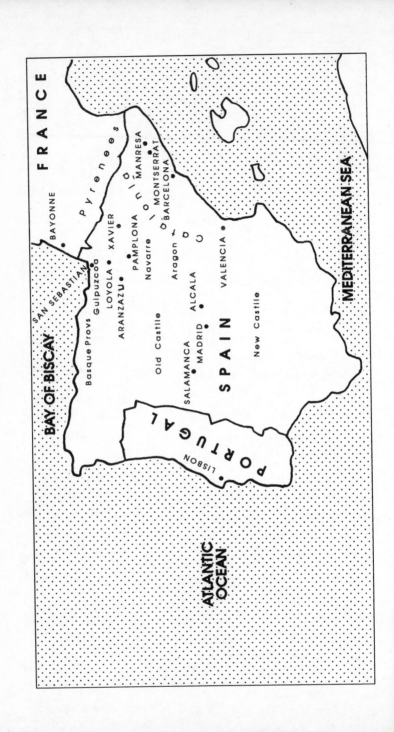

1

The knight

A letter to Ignatius of Loyola would probably have been addressed as follows: Don Inigo Lopez, Loyola, Azpeitia, Guipuzcoa, Spain. *Lopez* is a family name, *Inigo* (which we shall explain later) the Christian name and *Loyola* the name of his home. *Azpeitia* is the nearest town and *Guipuzcoa* the province in north-west Spain where it is situated. Inigo is often called "Spanish" but he really belongs to a race of people, the Basques, who live partly in Spain and partly in France amongst the Pyrenean mountains bordering the south-eastern shores of the famous Bay of Biscay. They were, and still are, ruled either by France or Spain, depending on which side of the border they live: nowadays they would much prefer to rule themselves. Inigo and his family could be called "Spanish Basques" and they, like their ancestors, were unfailingly loyal to the Spanish king.

Many small wars were fought in those days along the frontier, especially that of Navarre, the neighbouring province to Guipuzcoa, the French invading and the Spaniards driving them back, usually with one or other Loyola in the thick of the fight. In one of these wars the town of Pamplona in Navarre was captured from the French by the Spaniards, but the people of the town, disliking the Spaniards, wanted the French back. When the latter were preparing to retake the town, Inigo was sent to encourage the Spanish garrison, because he had already shown himself to be a good leader of men, able to persuade others to follow him. On his arrival he could have come to grief simply walking about the streets of Pamplona, for some pro-French citizens spotted him, attacked him and forced him against a wall; they quickly scattered when he pulled his dagger and threatened them. Other Spaniards rallied round, not so much to help Inigo chase off his attackers as to stop him starting a major riot in which they might all easily have been killed.

Before long the French attack began, twelve thousand infantry and twenty-nine cannon against one thousand men and nineteen cannon. The town itself was soon occupied but the Spanish garrison in the citadel hesitated whether to surrender without a fight or to face a siege. The French terms for surrender were too humiliating for Inigo, whose pride could not face the shame and dishonour of giving in just to save their skins.

"It must be defence or death", he shouted. "Honour comes first."

At length he persuaded the Governor of the citadel and the other officers to stay and hold their ground. Inigo now prepared to die fighting; he also prepared his soul by Confession, not to a priest, for there was no chaplain present, but to a comrade-in-arms in the Lady Chapel of the citadel.

The French plan was not to try and force their way by hand-to-hand fighting but just to besiege and bombard the fortifications till the garrison surrendered through want of men, ammunition and food. The enemy could afford to wait; all the Spaniards were able to do was to shoot off their cannon, but they did not have much to aim at, as the French were widely scattered inside the town. Inigo was frustrated since hand to hand fighting was all he wanted. He could only encourage his men who were firing, and himself dodge the enemy cannon-balls – which he managed to do for some six hours. Stone walls are made to resist cannon-balls smashing against them, but human legs are not, not even the legs of a brave man like Inigo. Later on he described what happened: "A cannon-ball struck one of his legs and shattered it completely, at the same time passing between his legs, it wounded the other gravely." The most serious wound was below the knee of the right leg which was broken.

Inigo was helpless, and so were the rest without his leadership. The white flag was raised, the garrison surrendered, the siege was over. Now the main French army marched off for other battles, whilst those left behind dealt with the conquered Spaniards. In those days of chivalry the winning side on the whole respected the losers, especially when these had fought gallantly against odds, saw that the wounded were looked after and let those not wounded go free, as long as they left the district. The French Commanding Officer took a special interest in Inigo and ordered his surgeons to do all they could for him by setting the broken bones and making him as comfortable as possible. When he was an old man Inigo still remembered the courtesy and kindness of his captors and how he had presented these with his shield, dagger and cuirass; he would not be needing these for some time.

Within the next fifteen days he was allowed to leave Pamplona. There was no such thing as a military hospital for him to go to, so the obvious place for the stretcher-party (which must have been quite a large one, and included Francis Xavier's cousin) to transport Inigo was his home at Loyola, though he had not actually lived there for years. By now his father was long dead and his second oldest brother Martin had inherited Loyola. Probably messengers went ahead on horseback, whilst Inigo travelled on a stretcher carried by relays of attendants. The distance is about fifty-five miles, the first part being through fairly open and level country, the second along steep and narrow mountain tracks and paths, constantly crossing rivers and streams, an awkward route at the best of times, but agonizing with the pain of a broken leg. It was fortunate that they were able to break the journey by staying for a week in one of the villages on the way.

At Loyola he found no brother waiting for him (he was still engaged trying to drive the French out of Spain), but his brother's wife Magdalena and her daughters were eager to take up the task of nursing Inigo, not realizing at the beginning how long it would be before he could walk again. They took him to the top of the house to his own old room with views towards the hills and valley of the Loyola countryside. The room is still there, complete with large oak beams supporting the roof, at which he must have gazed for hours on end thinking of his past life and planning what he would do when he recovered.

This is the place to say something about Inigo's family and home. He was born in 1491 (just one year before Christopher Columbus first sailed on the voyage that led him to America). The date of the defence of Pamplona was May 20th, 1521. Those who know some English history will remember that for the early part of those thirty years the king of England was Henry VII, and for the latter part Henry VIII. The corresponding rulers in Spain were Ferdinand and Isabella, followed by the Emperor Charles V.

Inigo was the youngest of a family of thirteen children; his father's name was Beltran and that of his mother, a woman of deep Catholic faith, was Marina. For Inigo's Baptism the family made a procession from Loyola to the church of St Sebastian in Azpeitia. He was given the name "Inigo" because it was popular among the Basques of the region, having belonged to a holy Benedictine abbot many years before. In his middle age Inigo of Loyola began signing his name "Ignatius", and by this name he was canonized and became known to posterity. We shall stick to "Inigo" till we reach the time when he changed it. The font in which he was baptized is still in use and has been given a cover with a small statue of Inigo on top and the following words inscribed below: "I was baptized here".

His parents decided that Inigo should have a nurse, not to come and live in the house, but take him to her own house a few hundred yards away. The woman chosen was Maria, the blacksmith's wife. It turned out to be a wise decision as Inigo's mother died not long after his birth. He grew up with the children of the family and their neighbours from the local farms, learnt to talk their Basque language, say their prayers, sing their songs, dance their dances, play their games and fish in the river running through the fields outside the house. He would, too, watch for hours as he grew older the blacksmith working at the forge, not just on horseshoes but on farm implements, armour and weapons.

Loyola is a beautiful place, set in a valley about two and a half miles long and only a quarter of a mile wide, room enough for a road and river, some houses and a few meadows and ploughed fields. On all sides mountains rise, so that from the centre it seems that there is no way out of the valley. However, at the south-western end the road squeezes through a gap at the village of Azcoitia, and at the opposite end road and river make their way through the town of Azpeitia and turn towards the Bay of Biscay. The area has as industries both iron mines and stone quarries. The hillsides, however, are dotted with whitewashed farmhouses and echo with the bells of cows and sheep.

By the time Inigo was seven his father brought him back permanently to the family house to continue his education as a member of a noble family. He will have heard talk of his other brothers: two had been killed fighting the French and a third had died in newly-discovered America. His own ambition must have been stirred to live up to the tradition of service to the king and to make a name for himself. Meanwhile he needed to study, not at school but with tutors. The subjects were: Handwriting (he was, in his own words, "a very good pen-man"), Spanish, Music and Singing, as well as Horsemanship and Fencing as he grew older. His father was always on the look-out for giving this son, so much younger than the rest of the family, a good start in life.

Now for a word about the house where the Loyola family lived. It was right in the middle of the valley and was called in Spanish a "Casa Torre", that is, a "Tower House". The name is appropriate, since the house looks like a large, solid, square church tower, standing by itself amongst the trees, four storeys high from the ground, with each side sixty feet long and the walls three feet thick. Over the main door there was, and still is, the coat of arms: a cauldron hanging on a chain with, on either side, a wolf standing on its hind legs wagging its tail and looking into the cauldron. On the ground-floor were the cellars and stables; on the first-floor the kitchen and servants' quarters; on the second the main living-rooms, the chapel and the parents' bedroom where Inigo was born; on the third, rooms for the rest of the family and for guests. In the time of Inigo's grandfather the local citizens, who did not like the Lopez family, attacked and badly damaged the Tower House. Grandfather Lopez was himself sent by the king to fight the Moors in a distant part of Spain. A few years later the same king allowed him back with permission to rebuild his house but without the battlements at roof level. This he did, using red brick for the top two storeys instead of stone. Inigo's room was in this rebuilt part. The whole house still stands intact, but can-

not be seen from a distance as it has been surrounded with the buildings of a Jesuit church and
College of St Ignatius.

When Inigo was about fourteen his father received a letter from an old friend of his family,
inviting him to send one of his sons to be educated
together with his own sons. This was a chance not
to be refused, for the writer of the letter was Don
Juan Velasquez, steward of the money and treas-
ures of the king, one of the most distinguished
men in the realm. Inigo travelled some four hundred
miles to the south to the home of Velasquez where
he met not only the sons of the family, but also
other young nobles from the Basque lands and
other provinces, all being trained as pages for
service in important households and even in the
king's court. Though Inigo was never himself
appointed a royal page, he would, as a member of
the Velasquez household, frequently be present at
court when his master was summoned by the king
on business.

As the king moved from one royal residence to
another, Velasquez and his retinue would become
familiar with various parts of Spain. The boys and
young men would gradually come to know how
the country was governed, how its wealth was used,
how courtiers behaved. They would develop in
themselves ideals of courtesy, honour, truthful-
ness and fidelity and they would see the kind of
opportunities that would be open to them for serving their country. They would take part in grand
ceremonies, wear fine clothes, watch the tournaments of the knights, admire the ladies of the court.
When not on duty the pages had many amuse-

ments amongst themselves, whether it was practical jokes, or dancing or singing to the lute, or becoming skilled at fencing and riding. No doubt they dreamt of the deeds of chivalry they would perform when they were men, imitating the heroes about whom they read in the only kind of book which Inigo enjoyed, romance and adventure. Whilst still in his teens Inigo once earned a good ticking-off from one of the older ladies of the court, his aunt: "Inigo, you'll never learn sense until someone gives you a good hiding."

From his late teens on Inigo started to fall in love. He was attracted by many women in these years and his day-dreams were filled with schemes of doing great deeds, such as rescuing them in distress. When in the mood, he would compose poems and set them to music on his lute. He never got married and in later years he felt ashamed of some of his behaviour towards women. Gradually his affection settled on one whom he described as "neither Countess nor Duchess, but above either" – in other words a Princess of the Royal Family. He may not actually have met her, but often saw her at court functions or took part in tournaments when she was a spectator.

After about ten years, all this life came to an end when, on the death of King Ferdinand, Don Juan Velasquez fell into disgrace for disobeying the orders of the new king, the Emperor Charles V. Soon Velasquez died, a ruined man. Inigo, as a result, had now at the age of twenty-six no job; he had also learnt a sad lesson, that wealth and importance can all too easily and suddenly be destroyed. It was Don Juan's widow who came to his rescue.

"Don Inigo," she said, "I know my husband valued your services and had a fine career in mind for you. There is nothing I can do for you here, but you are young and enthusiastic enough to make a fresh start. So I will give you a letter to a good friend of my husband and myself, the Duke of Najera, who has just been appointed Viceroy of Navarre. Life will be more exciting up there on the border with France, and you seem to me to be in need of a more active life. I am arranging for you to be given five hundred crowns and two horses as a farewell mark of friendship."

Inigo thanked her from his heart and vowed to be worthy of the chance she had given him. The Duke took him into his household as a "Gentleman-at-arms", whose tasks would include helping to quell any rebellions and to settle disputes, as well as playing his part in the fighting when war broke out on the frontier. He was not a full-time soldier, but, being highly skilled in the use of weapons (as he said long after to a fellow Jesuit) and in fact much enjoying this part of his duties, he was expected to command a company in attack or defence. Eventually, four years later he found himself at Pamplona, the chief town of Navarre, facing the French invaders.

2

"Holy books"

We have not forgotten the wounded Inigo lying on his bed in the upstairs room impatiently waiting for his broken leg to heal. To his family it was obvious that it was not healing, for he could put no weight on it at all. The doctors blamed the French surgeons who had set the bones and also the jolting that had occurred on the way home by stretcher.

"Don Inigo," they said, "we are afraid that your leg will be permanently deformed."

"I can't have that", he answered. "Is there nothing you can do?"

"There's just one thing, but we don't recommend it, the pain will be unbearable."

"What is it?" he asked.

"To break the bones again and re-set them?"

"Do it!"

"But..."

"No buts, do it! I can't fight or dance with a gammy leg."

They did it, and throughout the torture of the operation he made not a sound – just clenched his fists tight. Soon a fever came on. The doctors warned that he was now in danger of death; the priest came to give him the sacraments.

"What chances are there of his recovering?" his family asked.

"It's too soon to say", was the answer. "We can tell better in a few days."

The days passed with no improvement, then the doctors said, "Midnight tonight will be the critical moment; if he hasn't improved by then, he's going to die."

To everyone's joy, he did improve, the danger passed and the fever died down. When he was able to speak again they told him how relieved they were.

"It's all due to St Peter", he exclaimed. "He's always been my favourite saint and he must have been looking after me. What day is it?"

"June 29th", they said.

"There," he answered, "the feast of Saints Peter and Paul."

Feeling so much better, Inigo began to think again of the day when, with his leg mended, he could resume his life as a knight. He was made the more eager when his brother returned from the war with the news that the Spaniards had recaptured Pamplona.

Then came a big disappointment: the bandages were taken off the wound, but his leg was still not right, for below the knee a bone stuck out, which meant that this leg was slightly shorter and Inigo would have a limp. Further, the lump would look ugly beneath the tights which men wore in those days. A proud man like Inigo could not put up with these disfigurements.

"That bit of bone must go", he told the surgeons.

"We *can* cut it away, but it will be far more painful than when we re-set the bones; you'll have to have a rack to stretch your leg back to its normal length. You will be weeks more in bed. Is it really worth it?"

"It is for me, so the sooner you start the better."

He now had his third operation (without anaesthetic) in three months, still without uttering a sound whilst it went on, though at times he fainted with the pain. He described it all as a "martyrdom".

After this Inigo had to endure many days of convalescence, in bed and daily feeling more and more bored. Like many healthy and active people he had probably never been really ill before, and as he began to improve, he also became restless, fretting for the energetic life he was used to. He asked Magdalena to bring him some books to read.

"I didn't know you Loyola men read books. I thought all that interested you was fighting", she said. "What sort of books?"

"You know, novels with adventure, chivalry, romance, love. That's the life I enjoy reading about."

Magdalena went off to look and eventually came back.

"No romances anywhere, I'm afraid, but I've brought you some books of mine (she was carrying some heavy, leather-bound volumes). They're holy books – try them."

"Holy books! What do I want with holy books?"

"There are no other books in the house. If you're so bored, it won't hurt you to look at them."

After a pause Inigo said, "Oh, all right, thank you for taking the trouble to bring them." Although he did not realize it then, that decision was to change Inigo's life entirely.

At first he ran his eye over the pages: they were quite hard even to read, for they were printed in the difficult kind of type of the early days of printing. Then something interesting caught his eye and he read on. What he was reading was either *The life of Christ* or *The lives of the saints* and bit by bit he became more engrossed. Soon he was for the first time struck by two truths. The first was that Jesus Christ was a King with a kingdom far more important than the Spanish king and his kingdom whom he had been serving. He felt the sort of challenge he had felt as a knight, only it was to dedicate himself somehow to Christ the King. The second truth was about the saints; what brave and marvellous people they were. He, Inigo, thought he was brave and tough, ready to put up with hardship and suffering; this was much more true of the saints, whether as hermits in caves in the desert, or martyrs, or men and women who gave up all their possessions to imitate Christ and lead others to him.

Here was another challenge. Why should not Inigo do what Francis of Assisi or Dominic, for example, had done? It was part of his character to rise to a challenge, and by degrees he fell to planning a new career for himself as a follower of Christ in the spirit of the saints. Yet, at times all the old attractions came back – the glory and pleasure of the knight's life, the feats of arms for the king he served or the lady he loved. In the end he decided to finish with his past life and give himself to the new adventure of serving God. It was only many years later that he chose actually to be a priest; his ambitions now were to become an unknown pilgrim, travel to Jerusalem and spend his life in imitation of Our Lord by living poorly and preaching about the kingdom of God. There is a tradition at Loyola, that the Devil, angry at "losing" Inigo, shook the Tower House to its foundations. There is certainly a distinct split visible running the outside walls!

So much for those boring books: Inigo hadn't been bored at all, and now, instead of wanting his leg cured so as to be able to return to the world of knights and ladies, and his career as a Gentleman-at-arms, he wanted to be fit in order to travel as far as possible from them, to dress poorly and do without money and possessions. As he worked out these ideas, Inigo was more and more certain that he needed the help of Our Lady. There was a special reason for this.

"One night," he wrote, "as I lay awake I seemed to see Our Lady holding the child Jesus. No words were spoken, but I knew in my heart that Mary wanted me to dedicate myself to her." In his daily life he always showed her special honour. He prayed often in the chapel in the house, where there were pictures of two scenes in her life. One was of Mary holding the dead body of Jesus, a favourite picture in the Loyola family; the other was the Angel Gabriel addressing Mary. This picture Inigo's sister-in-law, Magdalena, had received as a wedding present from Queen Isabella in whose household she had been a lady-in-waiting. By now Inigo had started a large notebook into which he copied passages from his reading putting the words of Christ in red ink and those of Our Lady in blue.

All this time he was learning to pray better, not

so much by saying fixed words as by thinking over events in the Gospels and the lives of the saints and trying to make himself present at each scene. He would be an extra person in the stable at Bethlehem, for example, or at the Last Supper, and would watch, listen and talk to those there. Once he was able to move about his room, he often gazed out of the window into the night sky (from one of the windows the Pole star was visible, standing above the high mountain, called "Star Mountain", which rises near the house). He marvelled at the stars and said that the sight of them comforted him and gave him great heart to serve God. When he was out and about again, he used to walk the short distance to the blacksmith's house to visit his nurse and her family. Near this house at the side of the road overlooking the river is a small monument with an inscription telling that here Inigo would sit on a bench and rest his leg, reciting the *Hail Holy Queen*. Then he would limp another short distance across the valley to a small chapel dedicated to Our Lady of Olaz.

Soon came the idea of starting his pilgrimage by visiting the famous Benedictine Abbey of Montserrat (near Barcelona on the other side of Spain) with its shrine of Our Lady. By late February, nine months after he had been wounded, Inigo was ready to travel. All this time he had kept his decisions to himself, fearing that his family, who had certainly noticed the change in his way of life, would try to talk him out of what he was planning. It is true they *were* afraid that, for instance, he might leave home to become a monk (neither he nor they could have guessed that he would end up starting a new religious order). One day his brother walked with him through the various parts of the Tower House trying to make him realize that all this might eventually belong to him, even though he was by so much the youngest brother. He wanted to bring home to Inigo that he would be letting the family down if he were not ready one day to inherit Loyola. Inigo's training at court stood him in good stead now, for one thing he had learnt was to say "no" with the greatest courtesy and to keep his secrets to himself without appearing rude. He merely said that he must go and visit the Duke of Najera, whose Gentleman-at-arms he still was, as he wanted to claim some money owed to him.

The pilgrimage to Jerusalem he had mapped out involved travelling by land eastwards across Spain to Barcelona, by boat to Italy, by land again to Rome and on to Venice and finally by boat to the Holy Land. He was going to travel under the protection of Our Lady and began by leaving Loyola dressed in the elegant attire of a nobleman, without his armour, but carrying sword and dagger, on horseback and accompanied by his priest brother and some servants. About twenty-five miles away he climbed up the snow-covered track to the monastery of Arantzazu and spent the night before the shrine of Our Lady in prayer. He did this, as he said, to repay the visit Our Lady had made to him one night during his illness. The statue here is similar to the one in Montserrat: Our Lady sits, crowned, on a throne, looking straight ahead and in her right hand holding a sphere which stands for the world, whilst her left arm is round the child Jesus who sits on her lap with his right hand raised in blessing (similar statues are seen in some English churches under the title of "Our Lady of Walsingham"). Having put himself under Our Lady's protection Inigo parted from his companions and rode on alone to the town where the Duke of Najera was living. Like Don Juan Velasquez on an earlier occasion, the Duke had recently been removed from his post as Viceroy and, as a result, was not exactly well off, but he nobly said that at least Inigo of Loyola was not to go unpaid. Indeed, he promised to secure for him an attractive appointment as a reward for his services before he was wounded. Again, Inigo refused with courtesy, but gratefully accepted the money and set off on the three hundred and fifty mile journey to Montserrat.

NOTES TO CHAPTERS 1 AND 2

TOWER HOUSE (see pages 19-20). Many years after Inigo's time – to be exact in 1683 – Maria Anna of Austria, queen of Philip IV of Spain, bought the Loyola House and lands from the family and gave them to the Jesuits to build a college, on condition that the Tower House was left as it was. She also gave the money for new buildings, including the magnificent Basilica of St Ignatius.

The Tower House has remained, including both the room in which Inigo was born and the top-floor one where he spent the months recovering from his wounds. In this room, now a chapel, there is a life-size statue showing Inigo half-sitting, half-lying on a couch and looking up to heaven at the moment when he dedicated himself to God. Nearby in a glass case there rest some copies of the "holy books". The remaining rooms are being restored as far as possible to their 16th century appearance.

Opening off the room where Inigo was born is the small family chapel ("oratory") which really has been kept much as it was when Inigo prayed there. The two pictures of Our Lady remain and any visitor may pray before them as Inigo did.

Just outside the door of the Tower House (now called "Casa Santa" or "Holy House") is a group of bronze figures showing Inigo on a stretcher being lowered to the ground by two servants, whilst a third greets him on his arrival home. On the opposite side another figure crouches to welcome him: it is his favourite hound, licking his hand but not wagging its tail, for its senses there is something wrong with his master.

Many people come from the neighbouring parts of Spain and France, from the rest of Europe, as well as from overseas countries. To welcome them there are Jesuit guides who speak between them a number of languages. Visitors see not only the buildings and rooms, but also pictures, documents, relics etc., connected with Inigo's life. There are two items of special interest. One is the "Diorama", that is, a series of small models with figures in groups representing events in Inigo's life from his boyhood to his death. The second item is a length of the belt which Ignatius used around the cassock he wore as a priest. It has been cut up and arranged to form the letters I H S.

The college buildings no longer have students. A part is used by the Jesuits who live there and carry out a variety of works (some part is used as a Retreat House (see page 20) and yet another for the staff of "Radio Popular de Loyola" which provides talks and religious services for the people of the Guipuzcoa province. For example, those unable to get to church can tune in every day to a Mass. In the Basilica and some of the chapels of the Casa Santa many weddings are celebrated, since the people of the area are happy to be married at the shrine of their patron saint. His name, with the spelling "Ignacio" ("Inaki" in Basque), is borne by many men in these parts.

STAR MOUNTAIN (see page 28). On the highest spot there is now a statue of St Ignatius gazing out, as it were at his old home, and the river, fields and woods where he spent his early years. He would also see the farmhouse of his boyhood, though it is not a smithy. In fact, a narrow-gauge railway line runs outside the back door.

The Chapel of Our Lady of Olaz near the Tower House is still in use (see page 28).

At Arantzazu the monastery church has been rebuilt; outside one of the doors a Latin tablet tells how the knight Inigo of Loyola made a vigil there before departing for the Holy Land (see page 29).

3

Mountain and cave

Montserrat means "saw mountain" or "tooth mountain", since its peaks jut up into the sky as though they were the teeth of an enormous saw. Inigo reached it after about three weeks on the road, and then had to climb two thousand feet up to the Abbey church. He had done some shopping at the end of his trek, buying a proper pilgrim's dress: an ankle-length coat made of grey sack-like material, a rope girdle, rope sandals, a staff and a wooden bowl (for begging either food or money). These he packed in his saddle-bag for the moment. He arrived at the monastery guest-house a few days before the important feast of the Annunciation, March 25th, and immediately made plans to go to Confession, but not in the fairly quick way we are used to, for during his reading and prayers he had seen more and more vividly how many great sins he had committed as a courtier and soldier. Now that he was starting a new life, he desired to put the old one behind him, so he spent three days preparing for Confession and making his resolution "to try not to sin again". Still dressed as a nobleman, he received the sacrament from one of the monks, whom he told of his plan.

He had read that knights would perform a "vigil of arms", that is, a night of prayer in church, before undertaking their new life, and he thought that he would do something similar. First, he took off his fine clothes and put on his pilgrim's dress – "the arms of Christ", as he called them. The clothes he no longer needed he gave to an extremely surprised beggar, one of many hoping for some gift from pilgrims. Next, he gave his mule to the monks, as his pilgrimage would be all on foot. His sword and dagger he hung before the altar of Our Lady beside many pilgrims' offerings. Last, he took his place in the church for his night of prayer, which he passed sometimes standing, sometimes kneeling, keeping as still as he could.

He was far from being alone, for many others had chosen to come and celebrate the Annunciation at the Abbey. Nor was he in the dark, for the altar of Our Lady was lit for the great occasion by a hundred gold and silver lamps, the gifts of popes, kings and queens, as well as by forty huge candles brought by people of the district. Perhaps they all provided a little warmth, much needed on a cold March night. It was not a silent night: for one thing, other pilgrims sang their hymns, for another, the monks entered at midnight to sing the psalms of their Office. A few hours later, at dawn, came the sung Mass of the Annunciation; then, full of joy and peace, down went Inigo from the mountain, a penniless pilgrim.

To cover the next stage of his pilgrimage, the thirty odd miles to the port of Barcelona, should have taken Inigo only a few days; it actually took eleven months. Let us see why, if we can. At the foot of Montserrat he turned north instead of southeast, for he was looking for a quiet place off the main road to spend a few days. He especially wanted to put into his note-book many fresh thoughts which had come to him both on his journey and at Montserrat. For instance, the monk who had heard his Confession had given him much advice and shown him new ways of praying. So he made his way along what he thought was a path off the beaten track towards a town called Manresa; soon however, he was overtaken by a servant from the Monastery, who asked,

"Are you one of the recent visitors to the Monastery?"

"Yes, why do you ask?"

"Did you by any chance give away some fine clothes to one of our beggars?"

"Yes, why do you ask?"

"Because when the police found him wearing them they wouldn't believe his story."

"Well, please tell them it's true."

Inigo felt really sorry for that poor man whom he had tried to help and who had ended up by being arrested.

At Manresa began a new event for Inigo, begging for his food and lodging. He had always been a proud man, and proud men do not enjoy begging, nor do they enjoy being laughed at by children in the streets and called "Old Father Sack". Inigo put up with the mockery because he felt it made him like Our Lord, who had been mocked and jeered at during his Passion. Some charitable people sent him food regularly, but this he usually gave away to other poor men who were living in the same place as he was, the Hostel of St Lucy. He would not sleep in a bed, saying he was used to sleeping on the ground. Another place where he stayed was the house of the Dominicans, where the friars gave him a cell of his own.

Writing in his note-book cannot have taken Inigo long, yet he stayed on at Manresa. What did he do all day? He spent many hours praying: at Mass in the great cathedral on top of its hill, as well as at the various chapels, shrines and crosses of this hilly town. Remembering his own long months in bed, he visited the sick in the hospitals and carried out whatever tasks they needed doing, however unpleasant. He talked about the things of God to people he met in the streets, and he began to make friends with the children, so that soon there was a new name for him – the "Holy Man". He thought of himself as "God's new soldier".

His life was hard, for he slept little and ate and drank little (once he fasted completely for a whole week). Normally he would have a good meal on Sundays only. He beat himself twice a day. As another way of overcoming his pride, he let his fine hair grow and grow without ever combing it, and let his nails grow, too. The handsomely-dressed knight who had ridden away from Loyola a few weeks before was unrecognizable now. By all this ill-treatment of himself he was trying to imitate the saints about whom he had read and to increase his sorrow for his sins. But it was too much for him: he fell ill and had to be nursed back to health more than once by a kind family. They persuaded him to dress himself more warmly, give up the long hair, wear a hat and cut his nails. In this way he learnt that ruining one's health does not please God, nor does turning oneself into a human scarecrow, for this can put off the very people you want to help.

One day, whilst wandering along outside the town walls on a path some one hundred feet above the river he came upon a row of caves, one of which he made his own secret place for times he wanted to be completely alone. It was deep, with a wide opening and a roof of slabs of stone, each jutting further forward than the one beneath. Here he was able to have some idea of life in the desert, which was one of the things he planned for himself in the Holy Land. He had a tough time in the cave, worrying about the sins of his past life, wondering how he could possibly keep up the new life, thinking that God had forgotten him, tempted by the devil to give up and go back to the old life at Loyola and in the service of the king. However, encouraged by some holy men he consulted and strengthened by God's grace, he chose to persevere.

During his long prayers God had begun to help Inigo to grasp better the truths in which Catholics believe. He had not had regular religious lessons as school-children have now, but he appreciated, to use his own words later to his companions, that "God was treating me as a school-master treats his pupils". He meant that God took him one stage at a time, not trying to fill him with knowledge all at once (pupils soon give up if they are made to do new work before they understand the old work, or if the teacher goes too fast). He had a number of visions, in which he saw, not God himself, but, for instance, a bright light: as he looked he found that he "understood" in his mind more clearly, perhaps, the three persons in one God, or how God made the world, or how Jesus is in the Host. He never forgot these visions. At the time he had them, the joy they gave him made him weep so much that he actually had to stop thinking about them in case he wept himself blind.

Later on we shall describe Inigo's book, the *Spiritual Exercises* – the special way he worked out for himself and other people to organize their lives for the greater glory of God and learn to imitate Our Lord. It was at Manresa that he began to explain these Exercises to people who came to talk to him, and whilst alone in the cave to write them down so as one day to make them into a book. At Manresa, too, Inigo was shown (in a way it is hard to describe) God's plan for him to form a group of companions to work for the Church. When these companions had founded the Jesuit Order, and Inigo was writing, about twenty years later, the document describing their way of life, he was often asked why he had put in some particular section.

"This is the way I saw it at Manresa", was always his answer.

The stay at Manresa, as it happened, was the third turning-point for Inigo. The first was Pamplona, when, instead of a glorious death or victory, he ended up a wounded soldier; the second was the Tower House at Loyola, where, instead of many pleasant hours with romantic novels, he read the holy books. Then came Manresa: instead of making a short stay en route for Barcelona, he spent eleven months, being trained as a recruit in the army of Christ the King. Because Inigo at Manresa received this preparation from God at the beginning of his new life, "Manresa" is the name given in many parts of the world to the houses where Jesuits start their own new life. Some of them even make a pilgrimage on foot across Spain (Loyola to Manresa) in the steps of their father, Inigo.

NOTES

MONTSERRAT (see pages 33-34). To reach the Abbey buildings of Montserrat today one either takes the same route as Inigo did – on foot, or by car, coach etc. – up the steep mountain road, or goes by cable-car, starting from Montserrat station on the line from Barcelona.

The buildings, which consist of church, monastery for the monks, guesthouse and choir-school, are not the ones standing in Inigo's time, as these were destroyed by Napoleon's troops fighting in Spain in the early nineteenth century; only the statue of Our Lady survived then. It is similar to the one at Arantzazu except that it is black, for the original brown wood in which it was carved has slowly been darkened over the centuries by the great quantity of smoke from the lamps and candles. It is about three feet high and is placed, not in a separate chapel, but well above the main altar in the apse of the church. Pilgrims who want to reach it queue up in one of the aisles, then slowly climb flights of steps till they come out on a ledge in front of the statue.

There are still many (small) red lamps in the church, as well as larger ones outside, lit by pilgrims and arranged in rows in a special shelter.

Inigo's sword, which remained for many years in the church, was later given to the Jesuit college in Barcelona. It is now said to be kept in the church of

Belem in the same city. Inigo is remembered at Montserrat by a chapel in the church dedicated to his honour. He would enjoy the singing of the *Hail Holy Queen* (*Salve Regina*, in Latin) by the famous choir in the crowded church every day at 1 p.m.

MANRESA (see pages 35-38). In 1522 Manresa was a small town of some four thousand inhabitants: now it has seventy thousand. The first impression of a visitor on coming out of the railway station is that the town is hilly and light brown. The cathedral is to the left, the Jesuit house, retreat house and church (containing the cave, now a chapel) straight ahead, on the far side of the River Cardoner, and the old Roman bridge familiar to Inigo to the right.

It was many years before the Jesuits got possession of the cave (which the inhabitants call "cova"). They made it into a chapel without altering its appearance apart from laying a smooth marble floor and making a window across the mouth. On one area of rock a piece of glass covers some small crosses carved on the stone by Inigo. The cave faces in the direction of Montserrat, not more than ten miles away, so that the "teeth" of that mountain may be picked out on a clear day.

Many of the other places in the town connected with Inigo survived into the present century, only to be destroyed in the Spanish Civil War, which raged from 1936 to 1939.

4

Lone pilgrim to Jerusalem

Going from Manresa to Barcelona in February 1523, just a year after he had left Loyola, Inigo started enquiring about ships to Italy, for he had to pass through Rome about Easter time to ask for the Pope's blessing on his pilgrimage. Of course, he had no money and would not accept any to pay for his passage. Whilst waiting he spent some time each day in church, and some in the hospitals. During Mass one day he was sitting among a group of children near the altar-steps when a lady in the congregation noticed him, his face all lit up as he listened to the readings and the sermon. She seemed to hear a voice saying to her, "Speak to him, speak to him!" She went home and told her husband, who said, "If you see him again, invite him to dinner."

When Inigo did go to dinner he explained his plans and his problem about getting a free passage. They didn't offer to pay for one, but promised to make arrangements with a sea-captain whom they knew. When this had been fixed, they told Inigo that the boat would sail in three days, and that meanwhile they would put together enough provisions for the voyage. "Thank you," he said, "but don't think me rude if I don't accept; I've promised God to beg my way and that includes food." His begging brought him some stale bread and also enough money to buy "ship's biscuit" (hard and tasteless); the little money he hadn't spent he left on a bench on the quayside.

In the harbour of Barcelona today there is a model of the ship (the "Santa Maria") in which Christopher Columbus sailed to explore the New World. It could well be that Inigo travelled in the same kind of ship. The voyage of five days due east across the Mediterranean took Inigo and some other travellers for Rome to the coast of Italy, about sixty miles south-east of Rome. This last part they walked, along one of the famous straight Roman roads. The journey was not quite as easy as it sounds because there had been an outbreak of plague in Italy, which made the "police" at each town and village most suspicious of strangers in case they were carrying the germs. Even when Inigo tried begging, people backed away from him as though he was either a ghost or a leper; what he didn't appreciate was that all the fasting at Manresa had made him skinny and unhealthy-looking. The other pilgrims consoled him saying, "If you really had the plague, you'd be dead by now!"

The first sign of Rome was the acqueducts, rows of half-ruined arches stretching across the countryside. The party reached the city at the beginning of Holy Week and Inigo found a good place to stay, a hostel for Spanish pilgrims in what is now called the Piazza Navona, more or less in the centre of Rome. Here he had all the advice he needed from fellow-countrymen about how to get the certificate, a sort of passport, for the Holy Land, how to attend an audience given by the Pope

(Adrian VI) and how to visit the seven most important churches. Not long ago a scholar, going through some old documents at the Vatican, came across the text of this certificate in the archives. These are the words (translated from Latin): "Inigo of Loyola, from the Diocese of Pamplona, is given permission to go on pilgrimage to the Holy Land: March 31st, 1523." No one could have guessed that, thirty years later, this pilgrim would be one of the best known men in Rome. During his fortnight's stay he will have heard that the Turkish navy was gradually conquering the eastern Mediterranean and thus threatening great danger to pilgrimage ships sailing towards the Holy Land. After one of their victories the Turks raised the cry, "On to Rome! We shall conquer Rome!" Luckily they never did.

Before Inigo could face the problem of the pilgrimage ship, there were four hundred more miles of walking; Rome to Venice was Inigo's first really long walk (Venice was the only port from which pilgrimage ships sailed). He had with him a present of some money, seven crowns, from friends he had made in Rome.

After one day's march, he began to be worried, not that the money wouldn't last, but because he was not keeping his resolution to beg his way day by day and trust in God to look after him. The next day he gave the crowns away one by one to beggars he met. It was a hard journey, partly for want of companionship; pilgrims usually travel in small or large groups, but Inigo wanted to be alone to show that he relied on God only and not on any human support.

In spite of spring weather, mountain passes still meant snow and swollen rivers (he had to cross the Appennine mountains somewhere). He was also constantly hungry and unwell, rarely had a good night's sleep and was slowed down by his limp. In spite of all this, he kept going, encouraged by Our Lord appearing to him with the words, "Inigo, keep your faith, nothing shall stand in your way."

When he reached Venice he needed all the comfort he could get, for he was thoroughly exhausted, with just enough money for one night in a hostel. After this, as he failed to beg any more money, he had to sleep on a stone bench in a covered passage outside the palace of the Doge (the ruler of Venice) – one can still see the benches. Begging in Venice was a special problem because his Italian was poor, and there were fewer Spaniards about than in Rome. However, once again God rewarded his trust, for one night he was woken up by some lanterns being waved about in front of his eyes. Slowly he was aware that he was being spoken to by a well-dressed man, a Senator of Venice.

"What is your name?" the Senator said.

"Inigo Lopez, of Loyola in Spain."

"I am Spanish," the Senator went on, "and I want you to come and stay at my house whilst you are in Venice."

"I don't understand," said Inigo, "God wants me to sleep here."

"No, he doesn't," said the Senator, "and I'll prove it. After I had gone to bed tonight, I heard a voice saying, 'What are you doing in your comfortable bed when my servant is sleeping on bare stones?' I got up, sent for my footmen and started looking:

you must be the man God meant, so no more arguing."

That night Inigo had a long and comfortable sleep, and he spent the following days in the house till his departure was arranged. Because of the danger from the Turks there was no official pilgrimage ship this summer. Instead, those wanting to reach the Holy Land could join the ordinary merchant ships taking some Venetian officials to the island of Cyprus, and hope to find other ships there for the last short stage of the voyage. The man who booked a place for Inigo on one of these boats sent him a message that he must go and be interviewed by the Doge, Andrea Gritti. Inigo explained to the latter why he wanted a free passage.

"You don't look very well", said the Doge, and ordered his doctor to examine Inigo.

"No wonder he doesn't look well, he's suffering from a severe fever."

"Is it safe for him to travel?" enquired the Doge.

"Perfectly safe, if he wants to be buried at sea."

Inigo did not want to be buried at sea, but he did want to travel.

"I'll be all right", he said. "I've been ill like this before and I will get over it because I trust in God."

There was a long pause.

"I will order it to be done", said the Doge. "The ship sails in three days; prepare yourself for the journey."

Alas, Inigo was even more sick when the ship put out into the Adriatic Sea, where there is a long swell from one shore to the other. But, as he had said, he recovered and survived the voyage of just over six weeks, being kindly treated by fellow-pilgrims who had brought great amounts of food and always invited him to share. He was not so well treated by the crew who plotted (unsuccessfully) to maroon him on an island, because he had often told them straight what he thought of their blasphemous language. After avoiding both the Turkish fleet and the pirate ships which cruised around the Mediterranean, and changing at Cyprus, the pilgrims landed at the only sizeable port in the Holy Land, Jaffa, at the end of August.

For once Inigo did not do the next part of the journey on foot, but with the other pilgrims rode on a (very uncomfortable) donkey, with an escort of Turkish soldiers, for the forty odd miles up the two thousand foot climb to Jerusalem, which took three days. We should explain here that the Turks keep coming into the story because they had conquered the Holy Land. They were of the Moslem religion, which they wanted to replace Christianity, but their rulers did allow Christians from other lands to come and visit and pray at the Holy Places, as long as they did not try to settle down. The Holy Places were looked after by the Franciscans, given this privilege by the Pope some centuries before during the Crusades. As for the Turks, they only lost control of the country in the present century.

Inigo and his fellow-pilgrims entered Jerusalem in procession, singing and praying. Inigo himself kissed the ground, as the Pope does nowadays when he lands in a country. People often ask, "Are Jerusalem and the other cities, towns and villages the same as they were in Jesus's time?" The answer is that no complete buildings are still standing and the main reason is that, in the wars that have occurred in those parts, ancient buildings got destroyed and city walls knocked down. When peace came, new buildings and walls arose, as well as special ones at places connected with the Gospel story. For instance, Calvary and Jesus's tomb were in the open air, but in the course of time a large church was built to cover both sites, and they are still so covered by the Church of the Holy Sepulchre. Similarly, churches have been built at Bethlehem, Nazareth, Cana and other places. So pilgrims can still be in the same places as Jesus was, but not in the same buildings, although here and there occur exceptions. The Temple at Jerusalem was destroyed by the Romans, but they left the huge platform of stone on which it rested. Many of these enormous stones are still visible and we know that they date back to Herod the Great, in whose reign Jesus was born. Outside the towns, the countryside, mountains, lakes and rivers have changed less, and here pilgrims have a much better idea of the landscape as it was in biblical times.

We might have expected Inigo to keep a diary in one of those notebooks of his, but he gives no details of the places they must have visited – the Church of the Holy Sepulchre, the garden of Gethsemane, Pilate's headquarters where Jesus was tried, the Way of the Cross. When his party went out of Jerusalem they walked or rode the five miles to Bethlehem to see the cave where Jesus was born. It is a small place, not much larger than an average-sized classroom, with a low roof and rough stone walls. Here, perhaps, Inigo was happier than anywhere else, and for the rest of his life this was his favourite gospel scene, because it made him think of Jesus's example of poverty and of how he showed his love for all men by becoming like them right from the beginning of his life.

The longer the pilgrimage went on, the more determined Inigo became to carry out his plan of remaining in the Holy Land to live in the same surroundings as Jesus and, like him, travel about preaching the gospel (not to Jews, but to the unbelieving Turks). He had decided on this back in Loyola as a result of reading the "holy books"; he also wanted to imitate as closely as possible the daily life of Jesus, for example, being poor, illtreated and mocked. Towards the end of the pilgrimage he made some enquiries from the Franciscans, who told him that only their Superior could discuss this with him.

"Then please lead me to him", said Inigo.

"He's away in Bethlehem, you'll have to wait." (They did not like to tell Inigo themselves that he had no hope of being allowed to stay.)

The days passed, and only on the last day of the fortnight did the Superior return and send for Inigo.

"My brethren tell me you have plans to stay on here. I'm sorry to disappoint you, but it is not wise for you to do as you wish: the Turks would not put up with it."

"But, Father, I've made up my mind, I'm staying, you can't stop me."

"I certainly can; I have authority from the Pope to excommunicate anyone who does not obey me. Do you want to see his letter?"

"No, Father, now I realize that it is not God's will for me to stay. Good-bye and thank you."

As it was good-bye to Jerusalem, too, Inigo could not resist a final visit to the Mount of Olives, alone, in spite of the rule that pilgrims must always go in groups. He wanted to say his last prayers at the place from which Our Lord had ascended to heaven. Here pilgrims were shown a piece of rock on which were said to be the footprints of Our Lord, the last place where he stood on earth. Inigo made his way past the guards at the city gate by holding out a knife – not to attack them, but as a bribe. He was soon missed and a search party sent out to haul him back; he did not mind, for he thought how like Our Lord he was, being arrested and dragged away. Back in the city he had to face the anger of the same Father Superior, and, no doubt, of his fellow-pilgrims, too.

Riding back down to the coast at Jaffa and the boat for Cyprus, he kept telling himself that one day he would come back to the Holy Land, this time with some companions and the full permission of the Pope to fulfil the ambition that had for the present been disappointed. As he went, his head was full of memories of all he had seen and done and felt, things impossible to forget, which would always help him in his prayers and his preaching, for he loved, as we have said before, imagining he was actually there whenever he thought about a gospel scene. Now he had truly walked in the footsteps of Jesus, Mary, Joseph and the Apostles and all the others about whom he had read in the "holy books".

NOTES

BETHLEHEM (see pages 47-48).From the early days Christians have honoured the cave of Bethlehem as Our Lord's birthplace. Over five hundred years after his time a church, still standing, was built over this cave. In the cave there are two small altars, under one of which there is a silver star on the floor surrounded by a Latin inscription meaning, "Here Jesus Christ was born of the Virgin Mary".

Behind some leather curtains hanging from the roof one can feel the rough, natural rock.

JERUSALEM (see page 46). (i) The sites of *Calvary* and the *Holy Sepulchre* (tomb) of Jesus were close together and thus fit inside the large basilica of the Holy Sepulchre. The Calvary chapel is raised about twelve feet above ground level and has three altars; the Holy Sepulchre chapel is at ground level: it will only hold about five people at a time. Elsewhere in this church is a chapel well below ground level in honour of the finding of the Cross by St Helena.

(ii) *The Stations of the Cross* procession finishes inside the Holy Sepulchre Basilica with Stations 10–14 ("Jesus is stripped" to "The burial"). The first nine Stations take place along a narrow street of old Jerusalem, the *Via Dolorosa* (the Road of Sorrow), with pilgrims pausing to pray at little chapels, each dedicated to one of the Stations.

(iii) There is a small church near the beginning of the *Via Dolorosa*, with an archway spanning the road, called the *"Ecce Homo"*, from the words of Pilate "Behold the man", spoken to the crowd as he showed them Our Lord wearing the purple garment and the crown of thorns.

MOUNT OF OLIVES (see pages 47, 49). (i) This is just outside Jerusalem to the east. At the bottom is Gethsemane, now a small walled garden with flowers, shrubs and some ancient olive trees, beside a large modern church. In front of its main altar is a section of bare rock which may have been the place where Our Lord in agony prayed and sweated blood.

(ii) At the top of the Mount of Olives is a small, round, domed chapel inside which is the piece of rock Inigo was so anxious to revisit on his last day in Jerusalem, so as to examine the footprints Our Lord is said to have left at the Ascension. The rock is a disappointment, for one can only make out a small hollow about the size of a foot – nothing like a clear footprint. No doubt it has been gradually worn by the touches of so many pilgrims over the centuries.

5

A schoolboy aged thirty-three

Back in Venice in mid-winter, January 1524, Inigo saw that he had reached another turning-point. He had carried out his plan of going to the Holy Land, but had been prevented from staying there; he did not want to go back to Loyola – what would he do there? In his heart of hearts he wanted simply to help others to get to know God, Our Lord and the saints as he had done himself. He had the special gift of being able to talk about these subjects attractively, and whenever he did so his listeners asked for more; they also began to imitate some of his practices, such as the poor way in which he dressed or the time he used to spend in church. Now that he had seen with his own eyes so many of the places of the gospel story he could talk even better.

It gradually dawned on him that it was not enough to be enthusiastic, he also needed to do some study, the kind that is followed by those who are training to be priests. As it was twenty years since he had studied with the tutors at Loyola, he would by now have forgotten any Latin he may have learnt, a subject he would need to know before starting the main course. It was obvious that he would have to begin at the bottom.

Spanish and Basque being the only languages

he knew well, Inigo must go back to his own country to start school. The route from Venice to Spain was overland right across northern Italy from east to west, and then by sea back to Barcelona. Before he left there was a problem: no money and hardly any clothes. What remained of the pilgrim's outfit was much the worse for wear after the voyage. A group of Spaniards in Venice befriended him and gave him money and a roll of cloth, which he used not to have a cloak made, but to wind round his waist. He had not gone far along the road when he noticed that war was still raging, and realized that a lone traveller like himself might look harmless, but might be arrested on suspicion of being a spy. Inigo, of course, had better things to do than spy either for the French or their enemies, but this did not stop his being arrested.

The first time, the officer questioning him took him for a fool, as Inigo's answers did not make sense, and told his men to release him. Later on he was arrested again and was asked, "Name?"

"Inigo of Loyola."

"You must be a Basque", came the answer. "I am a Basque myself, from Bayonne, on the French side of the mountains. I couldn't imprison another Basque."

Reaching the sea at Genoa, whom did he meet but the Admiral-in-chief of the Spanish galleys, who had once been a fellow-page with him in the household of Don Juan Velasquez and who now arranged Inigo's passage to Barcelona.

The only danger on the last lap, apart from the weather, was being chased by ships of the famous Genoese admiral Andrea Doria, who was fighting on the French side. The Spanish ship escaped and arrived at Barcelona during Lent, just about two years after Inigo had left Loyola.

Nowadays, there are special colleges for men of thirty-three or even older who want to study for the priesthood, but in the sixteenth century there weren't any. Inigo had to be coached by a tutor, but he couldn't start with him until he had done the work of Rudiments and Grammar in an ordinary boys school there in Barcelona. Having an "old man" in the class was good fun for the boys, but it wasn't such fun for Inigo to try and study in the way they did; he worked hard but made slow progress. Most pupils are easily distracted in class: so was Inigo, but in an unusual way. Sometimes he found himself praying, instead of learning, or having marvellous thoughts about God or Our Lord when he should have been thinking about Latin. When this happened he didn't gain much from the lesson. Another problem was private study, that is, homework. He would sometimes arrive in class and explain that he hadn't been able to study the previous evening.

"Why not?" asked the master.

"Well, I had to visit some sick people in hospital; I had run out of money, so I had to do some begging for my supper, and then I had all my prayers to say."

"You can't have it both ways", said the master. "If you try to fit in all those things it's really a waste of time studying at all." (He was giving Inigo his lessons free.)

"I need punishment", answered Inigo. "Beat me as you beat your other pupils."

"It is one thing to beat a boy, but another to beat a man."

"Then I will beat myself." He did.

At the end of two years his Latin was good enough for him to go to university; the one he chose was Alcala (not far from Madrid).

During these years Inigo was using a method he had been working out for helping people who came to him, the "Spiritual Exercises" which we mentioned earlier. When a pupil is being taught in the classroom he has an exercise book and a text book with "exercises" in it which he has to do. Here "exercises" means "practice" or "training" for the mind and memory. So, too, the pupil will go to the gymnasium for Physical Training, exercises to train his body, or to the playing-fields for coaching and practice in sport. Or he may go to choir or music practice. Now "Spiritual Exercises" are simply one way of training people (or people training themselves) to know, love and serve God better. We shall explain later how Inigo did this, and just add here that the conversations which he held with those who came to him were part of this spiritual training. His free-time during his years of study was partly spent in these conversations.

After a little over a year at Alcala, Inigo went on to the oldest university in Spain, Salamanca. His stay here lasted only a few months. Priests and others had for some time been criticizing him, saying a non-priest like Inigo should not be preaching.

"I'm not preaching", he said. "I'm just having spiritual conversations with men and women who want to talk to me: surely one Christian can talk to another about Jesus Christ without having to become a priest?"

There was no real answer to this, but he was asked another time, "What is in that book you carry about and show people?"

"Do you want to read it? Take it away and do so, as long as you give it back."

They took it, could find nothing to object to in it and brought it back.

"Give us an example", they said, "of the way you talk to your friends."

"Very well," he said, "this is my way of talking about the First Commandment." He then gave them an explanation that left those priests wishing they could do half as well in their own sermons. Even so, they still kept at him.

"You shouldn't really be giving others your Spiritual Exercises if you're not a priest."

He himself began to see some sense in their words, but he also saw that he was a marked man, always liable to be prevented from doing the good he wanted. Therefore he decided to leave Spain altogether and start afresh in France at the most famous place for learning, the University of Paris. It did not matter that he knew no French, for the text books and classes would be in Latin.

He first walked the three hundred miles to Barcelona, where he met some of the friends who had helped him before. When he announced his plan of going to Paris, walking right through France in the middle of winter, they did everything to dissuade him.

"There's still a war on between France and Spain," they told him, "and any lone Spaniards who are found by the French are put on spits and roasted alive."

"Those are only rumours," he answered, "in any case, when the French captured me at Pamplona some years ago they treated me with great chivalry."

One thing his Barcelona friends did persuade him to do was to accept some money to pay for his lodgings and university fees in Paris, so that he would not again have to spend valuable study time begging. He collected his things, including some rather heavy books, which he could not carry himself. These he loaded onto a donkey which he drove in front of him all the way up France, putting his trust in God to protect him. His letter back from Paris, which he reached on February 2nd, 1528, would have fitted easily onto a modern post-card: "Excellent journey – arrived safely – many thanks."

6

The beggar-student's friends

The University of Paris was, like many universities, a group of colleges all situated fairly near each other in one part of the city. Students chose a particular college in which to study and took lodgings either there or nearby. Inigo began by staying in an inn where there were a number of Spaniards, then sold his donkey and went to the College of Montaigu, which he had chosen for his studies. The first stage was yet more Latin, as he had become rather rusty; then he planned to tackle the other subjects in the proper order and persevere with them "until God should show him the next step": no "crash courses" for him.

He had not been at work for many weeks when he ran out of money, not because he had lost or spent what his Barcelona friends had given, but because someone else had spent it. He had asked a fellow-Spaniard, a man he had met at the inn and who seemed reliable, to be a sort of banker. Now when bills had to be paid, Inigo found this man and said, "I'll be needing some of that money you are looking after for me".

The man looked embarrassed and said nothing.

"Don't tell me you've forgotten", said Inigo.

"No, I couldn't forget a thing like that, but..."

"But what?"

"It's all gone!"

"Gone?"

"Yes, I thought you wouldn't be needing it for some time, so I used it to pay bills of my own; I was sure I'd find a way of getting some money to make up to you."

Most people would have been wild and called him a thief and a cheat, but Inigo took it calmly, although he saw that now it would be back to begging and the loss of study time.

He was able to find lodgings (free) at the Hospice of St James a mile or so from the college, but would still need money for food and fees. There was another problem: at the college the classes started at 5 a.m.(!) and ended at 7.30 p.m., but the doors at St James's were not opened till 6 a.m. and were locked at 6 p.m. Thus he lost at least two hours a day, as well as the time spent on walking to and fro. Inigo was advised that he should plan to do his begging away from Paris (there was too much competition inside the city from other poor students), and go as soon as possible for some weeks to Flanders (part of the modern Belgium) where he would find rich Spanish merchants in the famous cities of Bruges and Antwerp: they were only two hundred miles away. He was successful, for the Spaniards promised to send money regularly to Paris where Inigo could collect it when he wanted. For several years Inigo did the trip in the university vacations. Then the merchants made a suggestion.

"If you want to do really well," they said, "go to England; we can introduce you to friends in London who are richer than we are."

"How do I get there?"

"We'll arrange for the captain of one of the ships going from Antwerp to London to take you: it's just across the North Sea and up the Thames."

In London the Spanish merchants lived by the Thames on either side of the Tower, which must have become a familiar sight to Inigo as he wandered through the streets calling at different houses. Probably he would have tried to stay as a guest at a monastery (perhaps the Charterhouse); almost certainly he will have visited some of the famous city churches, including (old) St Paul's. He would not have had a guided tour of the Tower, still very much a prison. Some of the street scenes would be similar to what Edmund Campion saw twenty or so years later as a boy living and growing up in the city. The king was Henry VIII, who about this time was planning to divorce Queen Catherine of Aragon; the Lord Chancellor was Sir Thomas More, who in only a few years time was to die on Tower Green for his Faith, and become St Thomas More. Inigo obtained in London more money than ever before, and from this year on he did not have to make any further begging trips. He used his money partly for his own needs, but also to help other poor students whom he came across.

After a year and a half Inigo was qualified to start studying for the Master of Arts degree, and he moved to the College of Sainte Barbe. Leaving out a description of the subjects he did for the next three and a half years, we will give an account of some of his fellow-students. When he asked for lodgings, he was told that the cheapest method was to share with others. Space was found for him in rooms in the top storey of a tower where three other students were already sharing, all younger than Inigo and further ahead in their studies. The three, two from Spain and one from France, introduced themselves.

"I am Juan, from Valencia, and am to be your tutor."

"And I am Inigo Lopez, a Basque from Loyola."

Another said, "I am Francis, from the castle of Xavier, in Navarre."

"Then we are almost neighbours", remarked Inigo.

"I am Peter Favre," said the third, "from Savoy, where the Alps begin. I used to be a shepherd-boy."

No one could have guessed at this first meeting that Inigo, Francis and Peter were to be, in a few years time, the first three Jesuits, and all because they were brought together as poor students trying to save money by sharing quarters.

It was Peter Favre who originally got to know Inigo well, and told him that his home among the French Alps, not far from Mont Blanc, was a farm in a small hamlet three thousand feet above sea-level. He longed for education and eventually persuaded his parents to give him the chance of going to a Latin school run by a priest in a nearby town. He learnt enough to qualify to study at the University of Paris when he was nineteen, helped by money from his uncle, who was Prior of a monastery. Peter was a shy and gentle person who, when Inigo first met him, was trying to make up his mind what to do in life now that he had got his degree: should he become a doctor, a lawyer or a schoolmaster? Should he marry or become a monk or a priest? Slowly Inigo helped him to sort out these problems. Meanwhile Peter was given by Juan, the tutor, the task of helping Inigo with *his* problems, by being his coach in his studies. He would answer his difficulties, see that he revised regularly, show him what books to read and, in general, encourage this middle-aged pupil during the long years of study.

On his side, Inigo, soon realizing that Peter was poor, began to give him some of the money that he had collected on his begging expeditions; then, as time went on, he was able to advise Peter in his many worries and temptations, and also show him how to pray. As they became firm friends Inigo said to himself, "Peter is just the sort of man I'd like to have with me to share in my plan of helping people to learn about God: I'll see if I can slowly train him."

Francis Xavier was far more difficult to make friends with. He was extremely proud of belonging to a noble family, and could not understand how Inigo, also from a noble family, had given up everything, even to having to beg in the streets. He was polite enough but often tempted to make fun of him. His own idea of enjoying his leisure was parties and sport (he was a champion high jumper), and he could not see the point of the kind of life which Inigo lived. However, Inigo soon judged (we don't know how) that Francis, though quite a different character from Peter Favre, would be an equally good companion, and that if he, Inigo, were patient, he could make Francis into a friend.

Nothing much happened for the first year, at the

end of which Francis left the College of Sainte Barbe to go and live in another one, where he had been appointed a tutor. At once his expenses increased and he found himself short of money. As a new and unknown tutor he did not, to begin with, find many pupils, and therefore did not earn much in the way of fees. Not (yet) a person to go out begging, Francis was often at the end of his wits with worries about money. Somehow Inigo heard of this and soon found ways of helping him. He kept his eyes and ears open, and when he came across students wondering which tutor to choose, he would recommend "my friend, Master Francis Xavier". On other occasions some of Inigo's begging money found its way to Xavier.

Gradually Francis grew to appreciate better the "old man" whose quarters he had shared, and he began to come to him for advice. One piece of advice that Francis never forgot was Inigo's warning about some of the friends he used to go about with.

"They're not the right ones for you, Francis", Inigo said.

"Why? What's wrong with them? They're not doing me any harm."

"Wake up, Francis, before it's too late: bit by bit, the way they talk and behave will lead you away from the Catholic Faith."

"Oh, I hadn't thought of that, perhaps you're right: thank you for that advice."

Unlike Peter Favre, Francis had the ambition of obtaining an important post in the Church, such as that of a bishop. But Inigo knew in his bones that such a life was not the right one for him. Patiently he put before Francis his own plan of gathering a group of people to work for God. It was a long tussle, during which he often quoted Our Lord's words, "What does it profit a man if he gain the whole world and suffer the loss of his own soul?"

"Inigo, go away", said Francis, annoyed. "You're trying to frighten me. I want to be a bishop."

"You're putting it the wrong way round, you should be saying to yourself, 'Does God want me to be a bishop?'"

"Oh, I hadn't thought of that."

"Well, if you give me a chance, I can show you a way of finding out."

These arguments and conversations were spread over several years; in the end Francis did choose to follow Inigo's kind of life and become his companion, but not yet, as Inigo was still concentrating on his studies.

NOTE

FRANCIS XAVIER (see pages 61-64) takes his name from the family home, the castle of Xavier in Navarre, thirty miles east of Pamplona. The Xavier family were Basques, but supported the French against the Spaniards. Thus, two of Francis's brothers were in the French army besieging the citadel of Pamplona when Inigo was defending it in 1521; a Xavier cousin was in the party escorting the wounded Inigo back to Loyola. Francis himself, being the youngest of the family of six, and only fifteen at the time, was not of an age for military service. The family of Xavier (spelt Javier in Basque) was descended from the kings of Navarre.

7

"The Rock"

Now is the time to tell of some of Inigo's other activities and experiences during his stay. At one period, in Paris, he got into great trouble as a result of some students imitating the way in which he lived as a poor man; they made their life so simple that they practically gave up their studies. Naturally, their tutors and parents were furious when they heard about these young men copying the much older Spaniard, though it must be said that he had given them some encouragement. The Rector of the college decided to impose on Inigo the punishment of a public birching. This was to take place in the presence of all the students and professors: they were to do the "birching" by lining up in the college refectory, each armed with a sort of ferula or strap. The guilty person had to walk down a space cleared in the middle of them whilst they all had a slash at him as he passed.

When he was told that he would have to appear next morning in the refectory, Inigo was furious, not because he was afraid of the punishment (he was used to rough treatment just from himself), or because he felt disgraced (he had taught himself to accept humiliation to be like Our Lord), but because he thought it was unjust. It would make the whole university think that there was something wrong with his leading young men to try and imitate Our Lord. So, after spending the night praying, early in the morning he knocked on the door of the Rector, and asked for an interview. After a while the Rector gave his decision.

"Yes, Inigo, I think you are right, it would be unfair. The birching will be cancelled, but do persuade those young followers of yours to attend their classes and do their studies properly. You may go now... By the way, sometime I would like you to come and explain to me what you teach your followers: it sounds worth knowing."

Another experience concerned one of the professors: Inigo was friendly with him and thought he was a man whom he could teach how to serve God in the way he, Inigo, followed. The chance of persuading his friend never seemed to come, but one day Inigo went to his house and found him playing billiards (a French invention, a game Inigo had never seen). The professor pressed him to try his hand; to be polite, Inigo agreed, but added one condition.

"We must play for a stake", he said. "I suggest that if you win, you may ask me to do any service for you for one month; if I win, I can ask the same of you."

"Agreed", said the professor with a laugh.

But the joke was on him, for Inigo had a beginner's luck, the balls whizzed round the table and went into the right pockets, so that the game ended in a win for him.

"What are you going to ask me to do now?" said the loser, hoping Inigo would let him off.

"You will allow me to give you my Spiritual

Exercises; they take just about a month, and they will make a new man of you." Needless to say, they did.

Inigo eventually, at the age of forty-three, passed his final exam for the Arts degree, which took place at an unusual time, just after Christmas; because it was such a hard exam it was popularly called the "Rock". He was placed thirtieth and was now qualified to receive the title of "Master", i.e. he could officially teach the subjects he had been studying and be addressed as "Master Inigo". The words of the Chancellor of the University to Inigo were: "By the authority of the Apostles Peter and Paul I give you permission to teach... both at Paris and anywhere else in the world. In the name of the Father and of the Son and of the Holy Ghost. Amen."

He was given a certificate with these words written out in his own name. The secretaries who filled in the certificate thought that the Latin for INIGO must be IGNATIUS, which is what they wrote. It was an easy mistake to make, as there is a well-known saint of the early Church called by this name, and Inigo must have read about him in one of the "holy books". From now on Inigo became Ignatius (or Ignacio in Spanish) when he signed his letters or when others addressed him; from now on, too, we shall give him his Latin name.

Ignatius received not only his degree, but also a hat, the special teacher's hat called a "biretta" (priests used to wear this hat with their vestments until recently). Now, exams and certificates and hats cost money, and more money was needed for presents to his various teachers and for his share in the series of parties held in celebration. To pay for all this Ignatius had to borrow, so he wrote soon after to one of his friends in Barcelona, "I am completely broke: I need the Lord's help." No doubt his friend took the hint. Master Ignatius, as he now was, did not want to teach, but to study another subject, Theology, the last one needed before he could be ordained priest.

For Theology he went to classes with either the Franciscans or Dominicans. During the same months he gave the Spiritual Exercises in turn to each of the special friends he had made in Paris. We have mentioned Favre and Xavier, now we introduce four more. Three were Spaniards, Diego Lainez, Alphonso Salmeron and Nicholas Bobadilla, and the fourth a Portuguese, Simon Rodrigues. The whole group of seven had made a habit of meeting together every Sunday morning at a Carthusian monastery for Mass, followed by a discussion about their ambitions, advice from Ignatius and a picnic. Slowly it dawned on the others one by one (as it had already dawned on Favre and Xavier) that they wanted for themselves the same kind of life as Ignatius was leading: to be poor men dedicated to drawing others to know and serve Our Lord. Ignatius had often spoken about his pilgrimage to the Holy Land and his desire to go back and settle there. They, too, felt inspired to go with him.

In the course of these debates they made the following plans:

1. They would remain together as a group of friends. It was later that they fixed on the name of "Jesus"

as a title and called themselves "Companions of Jesus". When put into Latin this becomes "*Socii Jesu*", from which we have in English "Society of Jesus" and "Jesuit".

2. They would take a vow of poverty (not to have private possessions of their own), a vow of chastity (to remain unmarried) and a vow to go on pilgrimage to the Holy Land.

3. They would wait until all had finished their studies, and then, at a date to be decided, they would meet at Venice, to begin their pilgrimage.

4. In case they were prevented from going to the Holy Land, they would go to Rome and offer themselves to the Pope for whatever work he might decide.

The seven companions wasted no time about the second plan, the vows. Ignatius picked the day, August 15th, the feast of the Assumption of Our Lady. The place was a chapel outside the city on a hill called "Montmartre", from the Latin "Mons Martyrum", the hill of the martyrs, the martyrs being St Denis, the first Bishop of Paris, and his companions. So far, they had only one priest among them, Peter Favre, whose proper title was "Father Master Peter". The rest of the companions would be ordained after they had finished their studies. Favre, then, it was who said the Mass, and just before the Communion he turned round holding the Host. This was the moment for each to pronounce his vows. Although this ceremony did not make the seven into a religious order, all Jesuits ever since have regarded August 15th, 1534, as the first step towards the making of the Society of Jesus. After Mass they signed their names and went off – for a picnic. The little chapel no longer exists, but a convent now stands on the spot, not far from the famous Basilica of the Sacred Heart.

In the course of the following winter Ignatius became too ill to carry on with his course of Theology at Paris. As a result of the hard life he had lived for years, especially the way he had gone short of sleep and good food, he had developed a weak stomach, which often caused him great pain, sometimes for an hour, and at the worst for sixteen hours on end. His illness turned out to be a form of gallstone, for which none of his doctors could find a cure. This time the best they could suggest was a visit to his native country, in the hope that something in the air (and perhaps in the cooking) of his Basque homeland would help him to recover. Ignatius accepted this advice and his companions agreed. It was the spring of 1535.

He had studied now for eleven years, four in Spain and seven in Paris. His results had been average, rather than brilliant, but enough for what he needed. He had also found out by experience how important it is to have a proper syllabus for study and to take it stage by stage, rather than jump about from one topic to another. Further, there was not much about the problems of student life that he did not know by now. Lastly, he had gradually made the six friends we have talked about, friends who would not go their own ways when finished with university, as often happens, but who had pledged themselves to stay together. The plans he and they had worked out looked as far ahead as the next few years. They were content with that and did not try to see what lay beyond.

8

Loyola revisited

When he first went to Paris Ignatius had planned
to stay there "till God showed him the next step";
now he knew what it was. Thirteen years after
leaving Loyola he set off to revisit his country,
travelling the whole length of France down to the
Spanish border near the Atlantic. His friends in
Paris had insisted that a sick man could not be
allowed to walk five hundred miles.

Ignatius did not argue and, in pilgrim dress,
gratefully accepted the chestnut pony they had
bought to carry him and his precious books. It was
spring, and jogging along he already felt better
and started mapping out in his mind his stay in the
Basque country. He would avoid going to live with
his brother Martin and his family at Loyola itself;
instead he would find some poor lodgings in the
town of Azpeitia. Even there he would not rest as
a sick man would be expected to do, but would
preach to the people.

Ever since he had left the district to go on his
travels, he had felt more and more ashamed of the
wild and scandalous life he had led there as a young
man. With his brothers and friends he had given a
shocking example in the town, going about in a
gang, rioting, starting up fights, gambling and
generally making themselves objectionable. Now

he desired to do something to make up for this past behaviour.

Towards the end of the journey he reached Bayonne in south-west France, and whilst he was riding through the streets he was recognized by a man from the Loyola area, who on his return sent a message to Ignatius's brother telling him who was on the way. This was misleading, for Ignatius deliberately left the direct route to take a track through the hills that he remembered would lead him to Azpeitia without going past Loyola. He came to a spot that was notorious for concealing robbers: sure enough, two horsemen appeared round a bend in the path, rode towards and past him and then turned round and followed him. In the old days of sword and dagger Ignatius would have had no trouble in getting rid of them, but these were not the old days. The horsemen drew level, looked hard at him and then greeted him with great courtesy. They were servants sent by his brother to watch the routes to Loyola and escort Ignatius home when they found him. No doubt he was equally courteous in returning their welcome and enquired how his family were, but he was absolutely firm about not going to Loyola with them. "Thank you for your company," he said, "and thank my brother, but I shall find somewhere to stay in the town where he can easily find me. Good-bye."

The place in the town which he had in mind was a shelter for the poor on the bank of the river with the rather grand title of "Hospice of Santa Magdalena" (the building still exists). Here he had a small cell of his own on the first floor and joined the beggars and other poor men for his meals, which consisted of whatever he managed to get by begging. He must have felt really humiliated at begging in the streets of his native town, but it was his own choice. His brother also felt humiliated and disgraced that a member of the Lopez family of Loyola was associating with a crowd of beggars when he could have stayed with the family; he found Ignatius and told him what he thought of him. It did not make much difference, though Ignatius did agree to accept a bed and some bedclothes for his cell. He also welcomed an occasional visit from one or other of his nieces; on one particular occasion he asked for some wine, warmed up. When his niece came back he thanked her.

"It's not to drink," he said, "but for my back. Will you rub it gently into the sore places there?" She looked at his back.

"Uncle, what has happened?" she exclaimed. "Those sores are horrible."

No answer.

"Has someone been beating you?"

No answer.

"Have you... been beating yourself?"

No answer. In truth he had, often, as a penance for others.

Martin did not give up trying to persuade Ignatius to stay at home, but he always refused.

"I have not come back to live in comfort", he would say.

"Then what have you come back for?"

"To teach people here to repent of their sins."

This made Martin feel uncomfortable for the

life he himself was leading was not exactly holy. Before he began on the sinners Ignatius resolved to give special religious lessons every day for the children, as they did not have proper instruction. He mentioned this to Martin, who protested.

"You'll look silly, you're wasting your time; they just won't come."

"I'll be happy if only one comes", was Ignatius's reply. The numbers soon grew until one day, behind the group of children, he saw some adults, including Martin. He used to speak, of course, in his native Basque tongue which he hadn't used much in recent years.

His sermons for adults also brought crowds of people, first of all to the hospice, then as the numbers grew, to a neighbouring field, where they hoisted him onto the branch of a tree to make him more audible and visible. He felt that if his listeners could only be shown, as God had shown him, how to give up their sins, they really would start to live holier lives. His words set their hearts on fire, and, when he spoke of sin, they sat up and took notice, not minding how long he preached (perhaps three hours) for they didn't normally hear sermons like his.

He went to the parish priest with a suggestion.

"Why not have the church bells rung three times a day?"

"What for?"

"To remind people to pray for bad sinners."

The parish priest agreed and had the practice started; it went on for years afterwards, for Martin left enough money in his will to pay a bell-ringer. Martin did another service at Ignatius's request by sending weekly a dozen huge loaves of bread, baked in the Loyola ovens, to be shared amongst the poor who were too ashamed to beg.

Once Ignatius went to the mayor with another proposal.

"You ought to make proper arrangements for the poor of our town."

"That's a great problem", said the mayor. "There are so many poor."

"Ah, but not all are genuinely poor: some are too lazy to work and just pretend to be poor as they go round begging. You should make a list of punishments for that, and they'll soon stop." Mixing with beggars as he did, he had easily picked out the false from the genuine. Remembering his own bad habits of gambling (cards, dice, betting), Ignatius realized that many of the "poor" were those who had gambled away all their money. That made him go again to the mayor.

"Sir," he said, "you'd have far fewer poor people and everyone would be happier if you made a law for our town forbidding playing cards or dicing for money." This suggestion was accepted and it worked.

After two months of these activities, Ignatius became a sick man again, with fever and terrible stomach pains that made him roll about on his bed: even *he* called this a grave illness. However, it passed, and he made plans to leave Azpeitia and start a round of visits to the families of the companions he had left behind in Paris. Before departing, as he now felt well enough to continue travelling on foot, he made a present of his pony to the hospice where he had been staying (we read that it was still alive and well sixteen years later). Ignatius agreed to spend his last night at Loyola with his family; next morning Martin organized his departure.

"Inigo, what time would you like your horse to be ready?"

"Thank you," was the answer, "I don't need a horse, I'm going on foot."

"I can't have any brother of mine walking away from Loyola like a tramp."

Ignatius didn't insist, not wanting to end his stay with a family row; he accepted the horse and the escort of his brother and other relations as far as the frontier of the province of Guipuzcoa. There he was firm: he dismounted, said good-bye to them, gently refused the money they wanted to give him and walked off alone down the road into Navarre. He never came back to Loyola, but felt happy at the thought of the good he had been able to do during his three months stay.

Of all places the road led to Pamplona, where he had fought his last fight and received his wounds. However, he was not going there to revive old memories but because it was on the way to the house of Xavier's brother. Ignatius had promised Francis and all the Spanish companions that he would visit their families and deliver letters explaining what they had been doing these last years and what their plans were for the next few years. In the course of these travels he visited a certain noble lady whom he had known in his days at court and who was now the governess of the heir to the throne, Prince Philip, and his sisters.

Philip is interesting to us for two reasons. The

first is his marriage to Mary Tudor, Henry VIII's daughter and Queen of England from 1553 to 1558. The second is the fact that, over fifty years after Ignatius's visit it was he who, as King Philip II of Spain, despatched the Spanish Armada to invade England. A year or two before the Armada this same King Philip was talking to the artist whom he employed at court.

"Bring me your latest pictures," said the king, "you must have finished some whilst I have been away from Madrid."

The artist produced his pictures and the king looked at one in particular with the greatest interest, studying the details carefully.

"Don't tell me," he said, "but surely that is a Basque called Inigo of Loyola?"

"Yes," said the artist, "some of the Jesuits asked me to do it because they had not got a really good picture of their founder."

"Did you ever know him?", asked the king.

"No, but one of those who had known him showed me a likeness of his face and head made soon after he died, then came to my studio whenever I was painting and described Ignatius to me as I went along. I must say that I felt it was a challenge, and every so often I prayed to the holy man, 'Blessed Ignatius, help me to get your portrait right – A.M.D.G.'."

"I congratulate you", said the king. "It so happens that when I was a boy Inigo of Loyola visited my governess and I saw him. I recognize him easily from your painting; only he had more beard then than you have shown."

Walking from one place to another in the heat

78

of the Spanish summer Ignatius covered about five hundred miles, ending up at Valencia, from where he wanted to sail to Italy, en route for Venice. A citizen to whom he had been introduced and whom he asked for advice about the crossing exclaimed, "What! Sailing to Italy at this time of year? I don't recommend that."

"Why?" said Ignatius, "I've been to sea in bad weather before when I sailed back from the Holy Land."

"It's not just the weather I'm talking about," said the citizen. "It's Red-beard, he's prowling around the seas near here – surely you've heard of Red-beard?"

Ignatius had to admit that he had, for Red-beard was a Turkish pirate whom the Italians had given the name "Barbarossa" (barba = beard, rossa = red), but he was not moved, especially as he had heard that a sea-captain had offered him a free passage, so he embarked in early November for Genoa, six hundred miles away.

Once at sea they had not much time to worry about Red-beard, for all their attention was taken up by a storm so fierce that Ignatius felt certain that only a miracle could save them, particularly when the rudder broke. He wrote about this afterwards, "I prepared myself for death by examining my conscience. The thought of my sins did not frighten me now, but what did make me afraid was another thought: how good God had been to me and how badly I had repaid his goodness." Somehow the battered ship reached Genoa safely.

There remained the walk across Italy to Venice, a mere three hundred miles, starting over the northern Appennines, once more in winter. One experience he never forgot. "It was the worst anxiety and danger I ever went through", he told his friends, "for I lost my way and found myself plodding high above a river along a track which gradually became narrower and narrower, till I could walk no further; nor could I turn back. So I went down on my hands and knees and crawled, terrified because each time I moved a bit forward, I felt I was going to fall head first into the river far below. I did get through in the end, but it was a very long crawl."

He then came to the city of Bologna and, trying to find the best way in, he started along a little wooden bridge across the moat. This time he did fall into the slimy water in the sight of many onlookers, who had a good laugh when the mud-soaked stranger climbed onto the bank. In that state he began begging his way through the city; but he must have smelt too unpleasant for people to want to come near and he received nothing that day. Not surprisingly he fell ill again with the stomach pains, but he was able to stay at a Spanish college until he recovered and started eating properly. He arrived in Venice about Christmas (1535), was welcomed in one of the monasteries and settled down to finish the studies he had had to interrupt in Paris, studies which would finally qualify him to be ordained priest. He was getting on for forty-five.

NOTES

RELIGIOUS LESSONS FOR CHILDREN (pages 75, 98). When they had settled in Rome, Ignatius insisted that all Jesuits, himself included, should spend some time giving these lessons. Amongst his letters is a long one setting out his own method, which was to explain the Ten Commandments, the commandments of the Church, the sins and virtues, the sign of the Cross and Confession. If a sermon was included it was *short*. The lesson always ended with the words: "Love God with your whole heart, with your whole soul and with all your will."

THE PORTRAIT OF IGNATIUS (see page 78) described here was eventually hung in the main Jesuit house in Madrid, where it survived until both picture and house went up in flames during civil disturbances in 1931. Fortunately copies had been made, one of which now hangs in the Prado Museum in Madrid, although it has been much touched up.

9

Missing the boat

Ignatius spent the whole year 1536 living in the house of a learned and good man in Venice, for once not short of money, studying and giving the Spiritual Exercises. One person to whom he gave them was a young Spanish priest, Diego Hoces, who had recently returned from the Holy Land. The Exercises turned him, too, into a follower of Ignatius. The companions left behind in Paris had planned to finish their studies and leave the city at the beginning of the next year for their journey to meet Ignatius in Venice. Their leader, in so far as they needed one, was Favre. As the year 1536 passed, war broke out again between Spain and her allies and France, so that Paris gradually became a place where Spaniards, if not in danger, were not exactly popular. This made the companions decide, for the sake of the Spaniards amongst them, to leave for Venice two months early, in November. They arrived well before Ignatius expected, though he may have heard about the war and had an inkling that it might change the plans.

When they met, there were introductions to be made, for the six in Paris had been joined by three more. Their names were: Paschase Broët, a priest from the north of France; Claude le Jay, a young priest and a boyhood classmate of Favre in the

French Alps; Jean Codure, also from the French Alps. With these additions the companions now numbered eleven: six Spaniards, four Frenchmen and one Portuguese. After the introductions, Ignatius asked about the journey and the companions took it in turn to answer.

"We zig-zagged", said one.

"How do you mean?"

"We knew enough about the fighting", he went on, "to realize that if we took the shortest route south-east we should be certain to pass through the war-zone. Instead we started due east to reach neutral territory at the German border. We then could turn south towards Switzerland which we entered at Basel; here we turned east again towards Lake Constance and Austria; lastly we went south once more over the Alps into Italy and here we are."

"How did you manage for languages?"

Francis Xavier answered. "We agreed before we started, that if we were questioned by French officials or soldiers our French-speakers would do the talking and the rest remain silent, and vice versa if we had to deal with Spaniards. We had problems in the German-speaking areas, and we often missed our way. Now and then we came across someone who could direct us in Latin."

"When you were questioned, how did you answer?"

"We said we were students going on a pilgrimage. As you can see we're still wearing our student gowns, with fur hats, and we have staves and haversacks."

"What was the weather like?'

"Awful, but we've survived."

Another continued the account, telling of their daily routine.

"As three of us are priests, we were able to have Mass every day. While we walked along on the journey we either prayed silently or sang psalms and hymns, and then, at bed-time, we joined in thanking God for the blessings of the day."

"Where did you sleep?"

"At inns, for we had been given enough money in Paris to pay for a meal and a bed every night."

It is unlikely that they had been able to keep a count of the mileage they covered: it adds up to about six hundred and fifty miles, or eighty miles a week).

The early arrival in Venice (January instead of in March) meant that they had to have a programme for the next two months, to occupy the time whilst they waited for the roads through the Appennines to be clear for their journey to Rome to ask the Pope's permission for their pilgrimage to the Holy Land. Ignatius proposed that they should offer their services in two hospitals, those of the Incurables and of Saints John and Paul. The priests would act as chaplains to the sick, hearing Confessions, bringing Holy Communion, anointing the dying, comforting and praying with them. The non-priests were to be part orderlies, part nurses, washing and feeding the sick, making beds, cleaning and digging graves. The companions split into groups and took up residence in these hospitals for the next two months. These brilliant students were truly putting into practice their desire to help their neighbour, in particularly unpleasant surroundings, for the hospitals of the time had no notion of our ideas of hygiene and there was no limit to the hours each man might work, all the time in great risk of picking up infection.

They set off for Rome in mid-March, leaving behind Ignatius, who said, "It may be wiser for me not to be in the party: there are two men in Rome who may find ways of opposing our plans, as I have had differences of opinion with them. One is Cardinal Carafa whose disagreement with me was here in Venice last year; the other is Dr Ortiz who did not approve of some of the things I did in Paris a few years ago."

The journey was no pleasanter than Ignatius's one from Genoa to Venice: bad weather, bad roads, shortage of food (once they could only find the little nuts of pine cones for supper, tasty but not filling). It was Lent, the normal season for fasting (on every day except Sundays), so they accepted the hardships as their Lenten self-sacrifice.

In Rome they had a welcome surprise, for some of them were recognized by Dr Ortiz, now an ambassador. Instead of hostility, he showed warm interest in their plans and made all the arrangements for introducing them to Pope Paul III. For his part the Pope was delighted at the prospect of meeting some Christians who actually wanted to go and preach to the Turks (this was the plan of the companions once they reached the Holy Land). Most Christians at this time preferred either to fight against the Turks or to keep as far as possible from them.

Pope Paul told Dr Ortiz to invite the companions to dinner with him and some cardinals in Easter week. In case the companions thought they were going to have a banquet, Dr Ortiz explained that the Pope enjoyed having learned discussions and conversations during his meals. He expected the companions to provide these for him as they had all so recently been studying at the famous University of Paris.

The Pope was so impressed with their achievements that at the end he said, "I congratulate you on your learning, and I can see that you have just the gifts that the Church needs today. Is there any favour I can grant you?"

"Holy Father," said Favre, "we are grateful for your encouragement. We do have two requests: your permission for our pilgrimage to Jerusalem, and your authority for those of us who are not priests to be ordained before we go."

"I gladly grant your requests," answered the Pope, "and I will order the necessary documents to be prepared for you. Further, I grant you a donation of sixty ducats for your pilgrimage."

The companions received their documents and ducats later, as well as another two-hundred ducats collected partly by cardinals and partly by Spaniards living in Rome. They were careful to make a note of the names of all their benefactors so that they could pray for them individually at the Holy Places.

Back in Venice in May they reported their successes to Ignatius and set about preparing for their ordination. They wanted to be ready should a pilgrim ship sail during the summer, though the chances were slight, for the Turkish galleys off the coast of Italy had become more menacing every day. Two bishops were anxious to perform the ordination, and Ignatius had to use his tact in settling on the one he wanted. He was the Bishop of Arbe, who had a private chapel in his house in Venice. On the feast of the Birthday of St John the Baptist, June 24th, he ordained Ignatius, Xavier, Lainez, Bobadilla, Rodrigues and Codure as priests (Salmeron, who was below the minimum age, had to wait till October). It was a day of great joy, not least for the bishop, who said that he had never experienced such happiness at an ordination.

In our times a newly-ordained priest says his First Mass on the day after ordination, if possible in his own parish with his relatives present. The companions, being far from their homes and families, chose to make a long and thorough preparation for the event. They decided to go away from Venice in groups (not too far, in case that pilgrim ship became available) to places where they were not known to spend forty days in prayer. Then they would choose days for their First Masses and follow these with preaching and celebrating the sacraments. Ignatius found these days of prayer as comforting as the final weeks at Manresa; he did not, however, say his First Mass, keeping this, as he hoped, for the cave at Bethlehem when they should reach the Holy Land.

When it came to preaching, the companions were not embarrassed to walk into a street or square, throw their hats in the air and catch them time after time, until they had gathered an audience. They spoke in a mixture of their own language, Latin and the little Italian they had picked up, but people did not move off just because of the language difficulty. They watched and listened and found themselves moved to the love of God. After their sermons the companions did not have a collection, but they discovered that when next they went on a begging trip the people recognized them and were very ready to give money or food. It was now autumn 1537, a time at which they had planned to be in the Holy Land. Yet, they were still in Italy, and in Italy they would have to stay till further notice. In fact, not a single boat went from Venice to the Holy Land the whole of the summer.

NOTE

The companions always added at the end of their sermons an encouragement to those listening to go to Confession. On one occasion Lainez wrote from the city of Parma, where he was preaching, "Confessions are getting numerous – it's wonderful." Later on in Rome, Ignatius himself found that many among the nobility, diplomats and cardinals chose to go to Confession to him.

10

The path to Rome

Failure to go on their pilgrimage in 1537 forced the companions to make yet another alternative plan to see them through the winter of 1537-38 until the next chance of a boat came in the summer. Ignatius proposed as follows, "I've had word from Rome that the Pope has invited two of us, Lainez and Favre, to be professors at the University there; this time I intend to go with them. The other eight, I know, want to go on working as priests wherever they can. To help them decide where to go, I have a suggestion."

"What is it?" asked Salmeron.

"As you have all recently been students, you ought to be able to meet other students who are finishing their studies and try to attract some to join us, as you yourselves did."

"Does that mean that we go back to Paris?"

"No, I mean you to go to university towns here in northern Italy. As you preach, say Mass, hear Confessions and give the Spiritual Exercises, people are bound to become interested in your way of life and God may well inspire them to ask to join you."

"Have you any places in mind?"

"Not yet, so we had better talk about that now."

The result was that they chose four cities: Padua,

Ferrara, Bologna and Siena for their work until the spring.

Before splitting up, the companions had a discussion about the title they should use for their group. (We mentioned this on page 69 at the end of the account of their stay in Paris). They could have simply called themselves "Followers of Ignatius", but he would have none of that. "Go and pray about it," he said, "and you'll soon realize whose followers we really are." When the subject came up again they unanimously said, "Our only head is Jesus Christ, and we must have his name in our title: we propose 'Companions of Jesus'." This pleased Ignatius, and not long after they had separated, something happened on his journey to Rome which seemed God's way of showing that he approved of the title.

Ignatius had constantly prayed to Our Lady, "Mary, I beg you to find a place for me with your Son." On the last stage of the journey, in a wayside chapel at La Storta, about seven miles north of Rome, Ignatius had a vision of God the Father, and Jesus carrying his cross. Both of them were looking kindly at him, and the Father said to Jesus,

"I wish you to take this man as your servant."

Next, Jesus looked at Ignatius and said, "It is my will that you serve us."

Lastly, the Father said, "At Rome I will be favourable to you."

Ignatius was happy that his prayers to Our Lady had been answered: for the words of the Father and Son he took to mean that they wanted him to spend his life in sharing in Jesus's work of preaching and suffering to save mankind. The final words of the Father, "At Rome I will be favourable to you", puzzled Ignatius at the time, but he felt that God would help and support him in Rome. Perhaps he was also meant to understand that Rome, not Jerusalem, was the place where he was to serve God. Indeed, after he reached Rome some hours later, he never left it again for the remaining eighteen years of his life (except for some short journeys in Italy). Furthermore, Pope Paul had said to the companions at the end of one of their dinner discussions, "Why do you want so badly to go to Jerusalem? If you really desire to help God's Church, Italy itself is the best place to do it."

The companions passed through the walls of Rome by the Porta Flaminia along the road leading like an arrow straight to the heart of ancient Rome. No doubt they stayed at first at the Spanish hostel already mentioned, but they were soon offered lodgings in part of a villa on the outskirts, near what are now called the Spanish Steps. Here is an incident to show how poorly they lived. A few months later, when the companions were going through a period of unpopularity, the owner of the villa told his caretaker to keep an eye on them. He did and reported back to his master, "These are truly saintly men: although I gave them beds, they always sleep on mats on the floor, and any food I provide they give away to the poor."

Whilst Favre and Lainez started their work at the University, the one teaching about Scripture and the other about the Mass, Ignatius did not have a fixed programme. However, he soon found the chance to give various important people (including Ambassador Ortiz) his Spiritual Exercises;

these we promised in chapter 5 to explain more fully. This "training", as we called it, lasted for about four weeks, during which a person spent a number of hours each day on different kinds of prayer and on a meeting with his "guide", Ignatius. As four weeks is a long time to keep up one's concentration, a free day was put in after each of the first three weeks. Ignatius began by showing people how to discover their good and bad points in God's sight, and then guided them to find out how they could best serve God in the future. This they did by slowly going right through the life of Jesus in the Gospels, all the time trying to get to know him better so as to imitate him in their daily lives. The last prayer of the four weeks was always "Take, O Lord, and receive all my liberty..." (see Appendix 1).

Many men and women make the Spiritual Exercises today. Some do the full four weeks, others a shortened form of a week or even a weekend: they call this "making a retreat". A school retreat is one of these shortened forms. When Ignatius guided a person through the Exercises he would visit the individual at home, explain what he should do that day, help him with any difficulties and encourage him. If there was more than one person at a time, Ignatius was involved in much tramping round the streets of Rome every day, especially from that villa on the outskirts. He might have finished with the very long walks of his days as a pilgrim, but there were still many miles ahead of him in Rome.

In the spring of 1538 the companions, whom we left in northern Italy, joined those who were in

Rome, but they were one short, for Diego Hoces was dead. He had been with Codure in Padua, and had literally worked himself to death. Ignatius learnt of his death, not by a letter from Codure, but through the privilege of being shown at the time of his death his companion's soul going up to heaven surrounded by rays of light (this was whilst he was giving Ortiz the Exercises), and he wept for joy. Codure himself explained his own experience after Hoces's death:

"I'm sure you all remember," he said, "that our companion's face was not exactly handsome. But after his death I could not stop gazing at his face – he was like an angel."

As Venice was still at war with the Turks, it had become clear that the companions would "miss the boat" again. They all now realized that they must carry out their alternative plan, namely, to offer themselves to the Pope for any task he might ask them to do. He, for his part, had received good reports about them from the cities in northern Italy, and he must have been waiting for the moment to use the companions himself.

During the summer in Rome, they had been much criticized for not teaching the genuine Catholic faith, and Ignatius had spent many weeks seeing that they were fully cleared of this false accusation. Then, in November, they made their offer to the Pope. He accepted it gladly; he was also happy to receive back the money which he had presented to the companions the previous year for their Jerusalem pilgrimage.

Ignatius, who had still not said his First Mass, now chose a church in Rome called St Mary Major, the most important of those dedicated to Our Lady.

Many Roman churches possess relics of holy people or holy objects. Here the manger of the stable at Bethlehem was honoured at a special altar in a crypt. Near here, on Christmas night, exactly eighteen months after his ordination, Ignatius offered his First Mass surrounded by the companions. Once he started saying Mass regularly, Ignatius used to take much longer than priests usually do in preparing, actually saying Mass and praying afterwards in thanksgiving. God always seemed most real to him at Mass, and here, too, Jesus on the cross was very close. During Mass Ignatius used to pray especially about the situations and problems which were causing him most worry. If, whilst we were at Mass, we noticed the priest weeping and sobbing, we should wonder what was wrong, but nothing was wrong with Ignatius when he behaved like this; he was simply overcome with joy at the thought of God's goodness (see Appendix 4).

Shortly before offering themselves to the Pope, the companions moved into a house near the centre of the city. It was larger than their previous lodgings and was rumoured to have a ghost. Things did go bump in the night when the companions first moved in, but they were really too tired to take much notice. The larger house was needed because gradually numbers of young men were being accepted as "novices" and space had to be found for them with the companions. It was a large, ramshackle building and was most useful during the terrible winter of 1538-39, not for the companions themselves, but for all the people they wanted to help. For five months the country was in the grip of the fiercest frost ever known, not to mention storms of snow and thunder. Soon there was famine everywhere and hundreds were perishing from starvation as well as cold. One of the companions wrote afterwards, "Everywhere in the streets and squares the poor lay huddled, frozen to the bone and dying abandoned in the night... There was no one to care for them in their misery."

In this crisis the companions came to the rescue, gathering into their house those who were lying in the streets. The sick they put into their own beds, and for others they begged from their friends bundles of hay which they carried home on their heads through the streets. They managed at times to squeeze as many as four hundred into the house. They also came to the help of about two thousand others who were trapped in their own houses, assisting them with money given to Ignatius for the companions themselves. It surprised the Romans to see these learned priests caring so lovingly for the needs of their neighbour, and even some cardinals came at night to find out for themselves. As for the companions, what they were doing seemed only another way of imitating Our Lord, who, besides preaching and teaching, cared for the sick and fed the hungry.

11

The Pope accepts the Jesuits

After the worst of the winter of 1538-39 was over Ignatius spoke one evening to the companions.

"I have some good news: the Pope has taken us at our word and asked for Father Master Paschase (Broët) and Father Master Simon (Rodrigues) to go and work for him at a convent in Siena."

"Did the Pope say for how long?" asked Salmeron. "Shall we ever see Paschase again?"

"The answer to the first question is 'no', and to the second 'I don't know.' This brings me to an important decision we all have to make."

"You mean," continued Salmeron, "do we have to split up our group as the Pope gradually asks for more of us?"

"Exactly: we have called ourselves 'Companions of Jesus', but do we want to go on being companions of each other as well?"

"Yes we do!" they all replied together.

"Then, my friends," Ignatius went on, "we must become an official group or Religious Order in the Church. We don't want to join any of the existing orders like the Franciscans or Benedictines, do we?"

"No," said Lainez, "the work we want to do is different from theirs."

"This means," said Ignatius, "that we must agree

what sort of Order we want to be, put it all in writing, take it to the Pope and ask him to approve it."

"Then the sooner we start the better," said Xavier, "before the Pope asks for any more of us."

The above discussion showed that the companions wanted to be united even though scattered in different places. They would be like a family whose members might be living away from home but who still remained part of the family. For the next four months (until June 1539) they met every evening to talk and argue and eventually agree on what they would put into the document for the Pope. The main point they wanted to decide was whether to have an official leader whom they would promise to obey. So far Ignatius had been their unofficial leader and "father", but there had been no question of *having* to obey him. In the end they voted to have such an official leader, but they did not at this stage choose anyone.

They finished their meetings just in time, since around mid-summer two more (Favre and Lainez) were sent to northern Italy and another two (Bobadilla and Codure) southwards. This left only four in Rome: Ignatius, Xavier, le Jay and Salmeron. Ignatius worked on the document for the Pope, calling it a "Short Summary" of the Jesuit way of life. Here is a part of the first section:

> We have chosen to be called the Companions of Jesus and to fight under the flag of the Cross in the service of God in the Church. After taking the vows of poverty, chastity and obedience we vow to go wherever the Pope may send us, in

Europe or overseas, to defend and spread the true Faith. We will do this by preaching, teaching (including teaching children their religion), the Spiritual Exercises, saying Mass and giving the sacraments. We also want to work for those in prisons or hospitals and any others who are in need of help. All our tasks we will carry out free of charge.

When this summary was sent to the Pope in the autumn, a cardinal read it out to him. At the end the Pope said, "Yes, I approve of the Companions' description of their new Order. I can see the finger of God here." He meant that he was sure that they had been guided by the Holy Spirit in what they had decided. A messenger took the news straight to Ignatius and explained that the Pope would have his approval put in an official statement signed by himself. None of the companions thought that this would take long to arrive.

Then came an unexpected hitch, for the cardinal whose duty it was to compose the document (called a Papal Bull), did not himself agree with some of what the companions had said about their Order, and he was not afraid to say so to the Pope. The latter did not want to contradict him, and he asked another cardinal what he thought. His view, given after some time, was as follows: "What the companions have written is just and holy, BUT, in my opinion we don't need any more religious orders in the Church – we have quite enough as it is." Once again the Pope did not like to contradict a cardinal.

It was left to Ignatius and the other three companions to explain their idea of a religious order to the second cardinal, but he would not budge. At this, Ignatius, disappointed but not in despair, now realized that they must all pray and go on praying for the cardinal to change his mind. The actual prayer consisted of three thousand Masses to be offered by the companions and some friends. Ignatius also sent letters to important people in the cities where the companions were working asking them to write to the Pope in their support. The prayers were answered; the second cardinal did change his mind and agree to a new Order, provided the numbers were limited to sixty. As the companions were only just in double figures at the time, Ignatius accepted this limit. More than a year had elapsed since the Pope's original approval when, on September 27th, 1540, the official Bull was published. Even so, the companions went on saying their share of the Masses, although only three were in Rome, and Xavier and Rodrigues had already left on their mission to India.

Now the time had come to carry out as soon as possible two lines of action. The first was an election to decide who would be the official leader or head of the new Order. The usual word for such a person is "General", meaning the member who is in general charge of all the others. To remind him that he is not a military officer issuing commands, there is added in front the word "Father", which should make him realize that he and the other members together make up a family (women's orders use the words "Mother General"). So far the companions had taken it in turn to be "father" for a week at a time and none of them really had any ambition to be "Father General" for the rest of his life. However, this was the arrangement which they had agreed on and asked the Pope to approve.

It should have been fairly simple for them to hold the election soon, for there were only ten people to be candidates and the same ten to do the voting. But of these ten, only three were in Rome; four others were in various parts of Italy, two more on the way to India and one in Germany. So the three in Rome decided to summon those who were in Italy and ask Favre to send his vote from Germany by letter. Xavier and Rodrigues had left their votes signed and sealed before leaving Rome. It was not till shortly before Easter 1541 that the election took place. After three days of prayer each wrote down his choice, signed his own name and placed the voting-paper in an urn. They then prayed for three more days before counting the votes.

No one was surprised that all the votes (except his own) were for Ignatius. They were certainly surprised when he did not accept, saying that he was quite unworthy of the office. He asked them all to think and pray for three more days and then vote again. This they reluctantly did – with exactly the same result. Even then he was not satisfied. "I'll go away from the house for a few days prayer by myself," he announced, "consult the priest who usually hears my Confession and follow his advice." Sure enough the priest agreed with the companions.

"Father Ignatius," he said, "you must accept, for I'm convinced the Holy Spirit has been guiding your friends. After all, they did spend much time praying for light. If you refuse any longer it's not them you will be refusing but the Spirit." To this Ignatius agreed and thus became the first of the twenty-nine Jesuit Generals.

The second of the activities mentioned above was the pronouncing by the companions of their solemn vows as Jesuits. They now had to repeat publicly the vows of poverty and chastity (mentioned on page 69) as well as two vows of obedience, one to Ignatius as Father General, the other to obey the Pope whenever he ordered them to carry out some particular task. For this ceremony they went in a group to the Basilica of St Paul, which is built some distance outside the walls of ancient Rome. Here Ignatius said Mass and before receiving Holy Communion recited his own vows; he then received the vows of each in turn and gave him Holy Communion. They separated for a short time to pray privately, and finally all met in front of the High Altar to give each other the "sign of peace" – very enthusiastically. The day ended, as the day at Montmartre seven years before had ended, with a picnic.

It was nearly twenty years on from the day which Ignatius had been struck down at Pamplona. His long pilgrim years were now over.

NOTES TO CHAPTERS 10 AND 11

The "*haunted house*" (see page 94) still stands, about a quarter of a mile from the Gesù church (page 126), but at the time of writing this book we found both ends of the street in which it is situated closed off...

St John Lateran was the last church visited by the companions on the day of their vows. They then had their picnic – it could well have been taken on the long flight of steps leading up to the basilica, for many tired pilgrims and tourists today can be seen resting and having their lunch or supper here.

The *altar* where the companions pronounced their vows no longer exists, but a mosaic of Our Lady and Child which was near the altar has survived and is now in another part of the basilica.

The *chapel of Ignatius's vision* at La Storta (see page 90) survives right beside a busy main road into Rome, the Via Cassia. In the course of four hundred and fifty years it has been enlarged, restored, rebuilt (after being bombed in World War II) and restored again, this second time with a design on the tiled wall to recall the details of Ignatius's vision in 1537. The chapel is small and square, with space for only about twenty-five people.

12

What does Father General do?

Even though at the very beginning there were not many Jesuits for him to organize, Ignatius was not short of work. He worked for the Church in Rome itself; he wrote letters to his fellow-Jesuits scattered in various countries; he had to start writing the "Constitutions"; he always had the Spiritual Exercises to give. In this chapter we will give, not an actual letter to Francis Xavier, but one he might have written describing what he was doing in Rome and giving news about some of the companions. Then we will explain the Constitutions briefly.

LETTER TO
FATHER MASTER FRANCIS XAVIER
IN INDIA

Rome: September 1546

The peace of Christ.

When I found myself elected Father General by the votes of yourself and our other companions, I saw that my days of travelling were over and my hopes of going to the Holy Land or anywhere else to preach the Gospel were at an end. As I settled down to spend the rest of my life here in Rome, I soon saw that there was much good waiting to be done, and I remembered the Pope once saying to us that there was no need to go to Jerusalem to save souls, for we could do this equally well in Italy.

In these early years I had noticed various groups of people whom we could help. For instance, there were women and girls in moral danger: for them I founded houses where they could live in peace and safety and prepare for a good married life. Then I opened a house for Jews and Muslims to live whilst they were being instructed to become Christians. I also planned that the dying should be cared for by good Christian doctors. Besides giving the Spiritual Exercises and preaching (alas, my Italian is always getting mixed up with my Spanish), I give lessons in Religion to children in open-air squares and often notice their parents in the audience: I do wish sometimes that they would stop their sons throwing apples at me!

Every now and then the Pope sends for me, generally to ask for more of the companions to go on some particular mission. On one visit, when he asked me this, I stood before him in silence for what must have seemed a long while, so he said, "Aren't you going to obey me, Father Ignatius? Why don't you answer?"

"I'm thinking about two things", I replied. "First, I went through who might be able to do the work you ask, and I realized that not a single one is free to go... unless you wish me to recall some from places where I've sent them?"

"By no means," said the Pope, "I've had good reports about their work, and it must go on."

I looked at the Pope below the eyes and said, "Then I will tell you my other thought. I can only carry out your wishes in future if you will let me admit more men to become Jesuits. There are many waiting to join, and I say to each, 'By the Pope's command we are limited to sixty; we are full now, and all I can do is to put you on the waiting list. When a Jesuit dies, then I am free to admit someone in his place.'"

It was the Pope's turn to fall silent. Soon he said, "Father Ignatius, when I first saw your plans, I said to one of my cardinals, 'The finger of God is here.' Today I say it again, for God is showing me that this is the time to allow your Order to grow. From now on there will be no limit to the number you may admit."

Father Francis, you may not realize it, but your work and your letters are one of the reasons why we have so many more applying to become Jesuits. When your letters arrive here in Rome, they are translated, copied and read by young and old, not only in Rome but in other countries too. "What a multitude of gentiles," you once wrote, "they would become Christians if only there were priests to help them!"

In another letter you said, "If only some of the learned men of Europe would think whether they are using their talents properly, they might cry out to God and ask him to show them what to do, perhaps even to volunteer for the Indies."

Now you will want news of our companions from the early days. After you left us, Peter Favre had six exhausting years, constantly on the move on work given him by the Pope, preaching, giving the Spiritual Exercises and trying to make friends with the enemies of the Church. He divided his time between Germany, Spain and Portugal, and he made us Jesuits and our way of life known in those countries. In this way he attracted two important new members to join us, a Dutchman and a Spaniard. The Dutchman is Peter Canisius, who has been doing marvellous work to support the Catholics of Germany in standing firm in their Faith against heresy. The Spaniard is Francis Borgia, Duke of Gandia, Viceroy of Catalonia, a personal friend of the Emperor Charles V. Francis has given up his rank, family and possessions to become a Jesuit. Peter Favre himself was worn out by this summer of 1546 and died a holy death here in Rome only last month.

Even before you left us I was planning to send two of the companions to Ireland at the request of the Pope. The Irish had refused to accept the English king, Henry VIII, as head of the Church and rebelled. They were crushed and sent an S.O.S. to the Pope. I chose Paschase Broët and Alphonse Salmeron; the Pope appointed them as his "Nuncios" and they set off, begging their way, in the autumn of 1541. Taking ship from a port in the Netherlands for Edinburgh, they were twice forced onto the east coast of England. On arrival in Scotland they were granted an audience by King James V, who promised them letters of introduction to some of the Irish chiefs.

Some of the leading men in Scotland did their best to discourage the companions from the journey but although they did not know the language, they set off in February 1542, Salmeron saying that he would be ready to wear a kilt instead of his Jesuit gown if this would help them amongst the Irish. They had to give up after five weeks of constant travelling and much hardship, and returned to Scotland where their friends were amazed to see them reappear. "We thought you were gone for good", they said. For myself, I find one small comfort from this failure, namely, that two Jesuits have set foot in England, Scotland and Ireland. Maybe the time will come when men from these countries will start to join us.

As for Diego Lainez, I can give you only a sample of his activities. Over and above preaching, teaching (including lessons for young children and tramps) and visiting the poor and the sick, he also found himself at one stage attached to the Viceroy of Sicily as an army chaplain in North Africa. This included taking care of two hundred sick soldiers and looking after the money and other valuables of those who had gone into battle. Twice he has been sent by the Pope to help with the work of the Council of Trent (see page 115).

Claude le Jay, too, was at the Council of Trent, sent by a German archbishop. He also came to the notice of Ferdinand, King of the Romans, who keenly wanted him to be a bishop himself (in Trieste). Claude wrote to me in great distress because, as you know, one of the things we chose to avoid was being made bishops, for our wish was to remain simple priests. I've had my work cut out recently asking cardinals to help me prevent the King getting his way.

One other companion I must mention, although you will not know him, as he did not join us till four years after you left. He is a Spaniard, Juan Polanco, whom I intend to make my secretary (a post you yourself once held). He, too, studied at Paris, not long after we were there, and then came to Rome to work in one of the papal offices. Somehow he happened to meet Lainez, who guided him through the Spiritual Exercises. He became a Jesuit, but his family were not at all pleased, and one of them actually kidnapped him and kept him more or less a prisoner. I can tell you that now I was the one not pleased, and I had to use all my influence to have him released.

Entirely yours, without my being ever able to forget you.

Ignatius

How much his correspondents longed for his letters can be judged from what Francis Xavier wrote just before leaving Portugal for India, "When you write to us in the Indies, mention all my fellow-Jesuits in Europe *by name*, as it is most unlikely that we shall ever meet again... and write at great length, as it will be only once a year, so that we may have enough to read for eight days."

Francis was overjoyed when he did receive a letter from Ignatius, and he followed the advice he had given by writing enormously long letters back, describing all his travels, his hopes, his plans for going beyond India to Japan, the difficulties of a missionary's life, together with his successes and failures.

Posting these letters back to Europe was not easy: it is said that Francis once walked three hundred miles to find a boat sailing for Portugal. He never read Ignatius's last letter to him as he had died before it arrived. In one way this was especially sad, for in it Ignatius had ordered him to return to Europe and report to the King of Portugal and the Pope on the affairs of the Church in the Indies. If he had been able to do so, Ignatius and Francis would have met once more. In fact, news of Francis's death (in December 1552) did not reach Rome until over two years later.

THE CONSTITUTIONS

Ignatius often discussed the Constitutions with the companions who were in Rome; some of the subjects which actually came up may be put in the form of a dialogue between Ignatius and Pedro Ribadeneira, a young Spanish Jesuit, who lived in the same house as Ignatius for many years.

PEDRO: Father Ignatius, you are always talking about writing the Constitutions. What does that mean?

IGNATIUS: I am doing this because the Pope, when he signed the document approving the Jesuits, said that we must make up Constitutions, that is, we must have written rules like other Orders. I prefer to think of the Constitutions as what Jesuits are and how they live.

PEDRO: Do Orders have to have rules?

IGNATIUS: Originally I didn't think we needed any. From the early days in Paris onwards we all lived in harmony as a group, we discussed our way of life and we took a vote when we didn't all agree. We were a band of friends wanting to work for God, and friends don't need rules: all they need is charity and the guidance of the Holy Spirit.

PEDRO: You haven't answered my question...

IGNATIUS: I'm coming to it. The Pope and his advisers have convinced me that I should follow the founders of the older Orders like the Benedictines, Franciscans and Dominicans; they made rules and they were far more experienced than we are.

PEDRO: I thought that we Jesuits were trying to be different from the older Orders.

IGNATIUS: In many ways we are different. This the Pope has allowed, but he would not free us from making up our Constitutions. Though when we were only a few we managed without rules, the larger we become, the more necessary they will be.

PEDRO: You seem to be taking a long time.

IGNATIUS: I am; partly because I have so much else to do, partly because I want to get them right without having to keep changing them later.

Ignatius did not make much progress in writing the Constitutions until Polanco became his secretary in 1547. With his help he finished them by March 1552. "Finished" means that he had a complete document to show to other Jesuits for their comments. The real end came when he had used these to make alterations. Then he was able to send Fr Nadal with the final version to make it known in Spain and Portugal first, and then in other countries of Europe (see Appendix 2).

WHAT IS A JESUIT?
WHAT DO JESUITS DO?

The answers are partly given in the Short Summary which we quoted on page 97. Here we add a few explanations.

A Jesuit is one who is so grateful for all he has received from God that he wants in return to spend his life serving God by imitating the life and sufferings of Jesus Christ. This means that he desires to serve other people, too, for the love of God. Some of the ways of serving others are described in the Short Summary.

Like Our Lord, Jesuits give up their own possessions (and so, for example, do not ask for money for themselves for what they do); they give up family life; they give up the freedom to choose for themselves where to go and what work to do. They are available to be moved from place to place to do the same work, or to be changed from one kind of work to another, or even to spend their whole lives at the same task in one place.

The majority of Jesuits are priests. Early on, however, men came to Ignatius who wanted to live the Jesuit life without becoming priests. Although he realized that such men would not be able to do all the works listed in the Short Summary,

111

he saw that there was a great number of ways in which, according to their talents, they could help priests, and indeed carry out many tasks which priests could not. They came to be called "Brothers", took the same vows as priests, were given the same spiritual training and shared the same everyday life. They were chosen to work, for example, as farmers, sacristans in churches, architects, builders, masons, carpenters, artists, cooks, tailors, nurses, hall-porters, secretaries, librarians.

Their work has been important in all places where there are Jesuits, and especially on the missions. Of the many Jesuits who have been canonized or beatified, there are four brothers entitled "Saint" and over twenty entitled "Blessed".

NOTES

FRANCIS XAVIER needs a whole book to himself; here we only give a brief outline of his journeys as a missionary:

1540:   Rome to Portugal, the port of departure for India (see page 99).
1541-42: Voyage of thirteen months to India.
1542:   Arrival at Goa (two hundred miles south of Bombay).
1542-44: Missionary work and journeys in India.
1545-47: Mission to the Moluccas (the easternmost islands of Indonesia, south of the Philippines, north of Australia).
1549-51: In Japan.

1552:   December 3rd: Death. Aged forty-six. He
          was completely alone on a small island
          facing China, where he was planning to
          preach the Gospel. One great sadness of his
          missionary life was that he received news
          so rarely from the companions in Europe –
          in fact only five letters in ten years actually
          reached him.

DIEGO LAINEZ became the second Father General
after the death of Ignatius; (St) Francis Borgia became
the third (see pages 106-107).

Fr NADAL, mentioned right at the end of this chapter
(page 111), was not one of the original companions. In
one sense he nearly was, since he was a student at Paris
during Ignatius's time there. Ignatius would have
welcomed Nadal as a companion, but the latter refused. Some years later, however, he was sent a copy
of one of the letters of Francis Xavier, which set him
thinking again about Ignatius and the companions. He
came to Rome, was warmly received by Ignatius, made
the Spiritual Exercises and became a Jesuit. He in his
turn was responsible for others asking to join, so
successful was he in making the Constitutions known
in Spain. He was also a successful beggar for the Roman
College (see page 118) when it was so short of money
in the early years.

THE REFORMATION

The Reformation was not a single event, like a
famous battle or the signing of the Magna Carta; it did
not take place in one particular year; it was not carefully planned, like the destruction and rebuilding of a

house. On the contrary, the Reformation was spread over many years in the first half of the sixteenth century, and it happened for different reasons in different countries.

People "reform" themselves by, for instance, turning over a new leaf, that is, improving their behaviour and getting rid of bad habits, perhaps by listening to those who criticize them. People try to "reform" an organization like the Church by criticizing what they do not approve of or refusing to accept certain things which it teaches. Thus, in England during the early 1530's Henry VIII refused to accept the Pope as Head of the Church and rebelled against him. Ten years before Henry, Luther in Germany thought that some of his own ideas were the real truth, and so he preached them instead of the traditional teaching of the Church. Because Henry VIII, Luther, John Calvin and many others were in this way "protesting" the word "Protestant" came into use to describe them; the word "Catholic" was then used for those who remained loyal to the Pope.

Throughout its history the Church has constantly been reformed, but in the fifteenth and sixteenth centuries it particularly needed reforming because of the behaviour of many popes, bishops, priests, monks and nuns. These had become worldly or rich or immoral, and were neglecting their real job of looking after the flock of Christ – they were bad shepherds rather than good shepherds. As a result, many ordinary people were not being taught their faith and became careless about Mass and the Sacraments.

Inigo grew up in these times, and, after he had reformed his own life, set about both encouraging others to lead better lives and gathering companions to share this work with him.

Inigo and the companions thought obedience to the Pope to be important because many Christians, rulers and others, were rebelling against him. Soon Pope and bishops invited the companions to work in preaching and teaching in areas where Catholics were troubled by Protestant doctrines, above all in Germany, Switzerland and the Netherlands.

Pope Paul III gave the lead in reforming the Church from the inside by calling a Council, that is, a meeting of bishops and their advisers, to meet at Trent in the Italian Alps.

His aim was to proclaim the traditional truths of Christianity, answer the teachings of the Protestants and remove evil practices. Of the original companions Lainez, le Jay and Salmeron were either summoned or sent to this Council as advisers (Favre was also sent, but he died in Rome whilst waiting to set off). The meetings were spread over a long period between 1546 and 1563. By the end of the final session the Church had been truly reformed; Inigo's companions had played an important part in the Council's success.

The Jesuits who took part in the Council were learned men, loyal to the Pope but at the same time only too aware of what was wrong with the Church. Other Jesuits had the task of making known the decisions of the Council, both by preaching and teaching Catholics who were ignorant and by encouraging those who were being ill-treated by the enemies of the Faith. Whatever they did, they always stressed the value of going to Confession and Holy Communion often – not just once a year, as so many had been doing.

A good example of all this is the work of Peter Canisius (see page 106), who, after attending the Council himself, spent the next thirty years travelling over twenty thousand miles in Germany, Austria, Hungary, Bohemia and Poland. "Dear God," he used to say, "what a task it is to keep the Catholics in the ancient Faith!"

Canisius was the first Jesuit to write a book. One of his later books became what we call a "best seller".

This was *A Catechism of Christian Doctrine.* A "catechism" is a method of teaching by question and answer. For instance, "Who is Jesus Christ?" "Jesus Christ is God the Son made man for us." Canisius wrote the original in Latin, but it was soon translated into German and then many other languages. A book for young people, it came out in three editions, the first for older children (Short Catechism), the second for younger ones (Shorter Catechism) and the third for beginners (Very Short Catechism).

13

Jesuit colleges

"I thought at the beginning that we would always be on the move", Ignatius once said when he found himself being asked to open colleges. He realized that any Jesuits who took up this work would have to be more or less permanently tied down to one place: they could not be running a school or college for a few months and then close it and move on to something else. But, once Jesuits became known in various cities and countries, men of influence – bishops, ambassadors, the Pope himself – started sending requests for some of them to settle down and open colleges. This made Ignatius aware that there was a need in the Church which he had not originally thought of. Since the desire of the companions was to help their neighbour, they could not very well exclude education, especially as many of them were so well educated themselves.

We give a few examples. Francis Xavier in India was allowed to send some Jesuits in Goa to teach in a college for Hindu students; in Europe, Francis Borgia, Duke of Gandia in Spain, persuaded Ignatius to open not merely a college but an entire university; in Sicily, the Viceroy, a great friend of the Jesuits, begged that colleges be opened in Messina and Palermo. By the time of Ignatius's death there were in existence forty-seven colleges in Europe (e.g., in Italy, France, Germany, Spain and Portugal), four in India and three in Brazil.

However, not all Jesuits were in favour of teaching boys, and one critic wrote, "It is a most tedious, troublesome and anxious task to drive, teach and control a mob of boys, who by nature are giddy, restless, garrulous and lazy creatures... their teachers lead a very hard life, fritter away their strength and lose their health... attending to childish trifles of no consequence." In other words, this work was not worthy of graduates of the University of Paris. On the other hand, Pedro Ribadaneira did not agree. His opinion was, "I doubt whether any other of our works has given greater service to God than the education of youth."

In 1551 Ignatius actually founded a college himself under the name of the "Roman College", so called not because the pupils would be inhabitants of Rome, but in order to provide in the Pope's own city a college and university at his service. Students were to be of various nationalities and would receive both a secondary and university education to send them back to their countries equipped to be loyal and well-trained Catholics. At the beginning the masters and professors consisted of Jesuits resident in Rome, but Ignatius's plan was to appoint the best teachers he could find from any country. Thus the Roman College would be truly international.

On the day of opening a notice was posted on the door: COLLEGE OF GRAMMAR, CHRISTIAN DOCTRINE AND HUMANITIES. FREE. "Free" really meant that no fees would be charged, in accordance with what the companions had said in the Short Summary given to the Pope (see page 97). Ignatius put all his trust in God to inspire people with money to sponsor the college. The wealthy Francis Borgia, mentioned above, gave a large enough donation to cover the early stages (for sixty boys and fifteen staff), but not many others, including the Pope, imitated him, so that frequently there was hardly any money in the safe, and the students, whilst getting their education free, were not being given much else. This shortage of funds, added to increasing numbers of students, made life difficult for the first thirty years, until in 1584 Pope Gregory XIII provided enough money for new buildings and guaranteed the fees of two hundred students. In his honour the College was renamed "Gregorian University" and it still flourishes.

England was not included amongst the countries of Europe where Jesuit colleges were founded (see page 118) because, after Henry VIII's break with Rome, there was no question of English Catholics being able to invite Jesuits to come to England for any purpose at all.

It was not until about the middle of the reign of Queen Elizabeth that the Pope sent Jesuits to England, to work secretly for the persecuted Catholics. The task of Edmund Campion, Robert Persons and the other missionary priests was to go round the country, constantly on the move (in disguise) from one Catholic house to another. They would say Mass, preach, give the Sacraments and support in all possible ways those suffering for their Faith.

After Campion was martyred in 1581, his companion on the mission, Persons, returned to the Continent and began to plan a college where boys from England could receive a full Catholic education. He chose a town in northern France, St-Omer, then part of the Spanish Netherlands, and there founded a college in 1593. Some two hundred years later, in the early years of the French Revolution, this English school was forced to migrate and settle in England at Stonyhurst in Lancashire. In the course of the nineteenth and early twentieth centuries a whole series of Jesuit schools, day and boarding, came into existence in the British Isles and in some of the overseas possessions.

NOTE

For a year or so during the reign of the Catholic James II in England a Jesuit day-school existed in London, in the Savoy area. However, it did not survive after the departure of the king into exile in 1688.

14

Living with Father Ignatius:
1541–1556

Before describing how the companions lived with Father Ignatius, let us explain exactly where they lived after settling in the haunted house in 1538. Three years later, in the year in which Ignatius was elected Father General, they were given a "crumbling old house" just behind one of the Pope's residences (the Palazzo San Marco), and very near the Church of Our Lady of the Way (Madonna della Strada), Ignatius's favourite Roman church. This became the first of all Jesuit churches in the following year, when the Pope gave it to the companions. In 1544, right beside the church, they built their own house, which remained in use till the end of the century, and was described by a friend as "dumpy, rather like a shack". Here Ignatius lived for the last twelve years of his life, and here he died.

Compared with his years as a pilgrim, Ignatius spent the years at Rome almost entirely at home, continuously working at the tasks named in chapter 12 (see page 103). Whatever the business of any particular day, he always spent several hours in prayer, both fixed prayers, such as his Mass and the other regular prayers of a priest, and his more private prayers, which he said either early in the morning or late at night (he did not sleep for many hours). In the course of the day he often prayed at odd moments, keeping on his desk a copy of the New Testament and a prayer-book called *The Imitation of Christ*. He had another way of praying, too, which he called "looking for God in all things"; that is, he trained himself to let things and people remind him of God. Thus, the sun, moon and stars led him to the beauty of God, and the sight of other human beings to the goodness of God in creating them and sending his Son to save them. He was fond of saying, "We should not think of God as far off in heaven, for all the time he is busy with the created world here below".

Anyone seeing Ignatius among the other Jesuits in the house, would not know from his dress that he was the Father General. Of course, he no longer wore the pilgrim garments, but he and the companions had decided that they would all dress in the same way, and that they would not design a special uniform just because other Orders had one. They wanted to dress like ordinary priests with a black cassock and a belt round the waist when they were inside the house, and a long cloak and broad-brimmed black hat when they went out. Ignatius himself needed an extra layer of cloth to protect his weak stomach, slippers for his feet and a cane to help his limp.

There are pictures, statues and medals of Ignatius in all kinds of postures – as a soldier, a beggar, a pilgrim, a priest. None of these brings out fully how he looked to his companions. This was well put in one sentence by his great friend in Rome (not a Jesuit), St Philip Neri, who described him as "the little Spaniard with a limp and shining eyes". Ignatius was not much more than five feet in height, but he was sturdily and robustly built (above all in his younger days). In his pilgrim years, in spite of his shabby dress he seemed to those whom he met to be so dignified that they guessed he must be nobly born. In the last years he had lost much of his hair, which was becoming dark, flecked with grey. Down the sides of his face and along his jaw went a slight beard, but only as far as his chin; he wore a moustache. His nose was aquiline, still a feature of the Basque race.

Because of his weak stomach Ignatius was told by his doctors to keep to certain kinds of food. One suggested, among other items, chicken, pigeon, veal, roasted kid, soup from meat, dried figs, roast apples and nougat candy. One wonders whether he actually kept to this diet, even though he was always strict about Jesuits obeying the doctor. Whatever the menu, there were two meals for the community, the main one about the middle of the morning and the supper at 6 or 7 p.m. Ignatius usually ate in his own rooms, not alone but either with one of the companions so as to discuss business, or with someone who had just arrived for a stay so as to hear his news, or with officials and friends who had come to see him.

We shall now try and get an idea of the impression Ignatius made on those who lived with him, by a conversation between a Fleming and a Spaniard, discussing their days in the house in Rome.

FLEMING: What do you remember best?
SPANIARD: Oh, the pleasant atmosphere when

Ignatius was amongst us. We all loved him and he had a way of making us feel that in return he had a special love for each individual.

FLEMING: Yes, and with that went his Spanish courtesy and charm. I was not surprised to learn that he had spent some of his youth learning the manners of a courtier.

SPANIARD: When you met him about the house his face was shining, he looked cheerful and often seemed to be laughing to himself – not at some secret joke, but simply because he enjoyed being alive, surrounded by his fellow-Jesuits. He liked a joke, and you never knew when he would start teasing you. There was Benedict, a large Italian with a big appetite. Ignatius would say, when he was at dinner with us, "Benedetto, come and sit near me, I do enjoy watching a man really relishing a meal, especially if I don't feel like eating myself."

FLEMING: He would try anything to cheer someone up. There was a rather gloomy priest, who responded to no one's efforts. Ignatius said, "Come, Father, can't you suggest anything I could do for you?" The only answer was a grunt. Ignatius persisted, "Say what you would like and I will do it." This sounded like a challenge, so the priest said, "Sing for me: you're a Basque, you have famous folk songs."

One or two of the songs of his youth came back to Ignatius and he sang them in a pleasant voice. "Does that make you feel better?" he asked.

"A bit," replied the other grudgingly, "but I'd feel really better if you did me a Basque dance."

The elderly Basque, limp and all, went through a dance routine that he had probably never done since he first got his wound.

SPANIARD: Then there was the Father Minister (in charge of catering) who had been out to dine one evening with a cardinal and was describing to the companions the feast he had enjoyed.

"Father," said Ignatius, "was that really the menu? Then you should give your brethren the same one day."

"But we could never afford it!"

"You must find the money and give us as good a meal as you had."

Ignatius was not really serious, but it did make the Father Minister realize that, if he could dine with a cardinal, then his fellow-Jesuits deserved more than the sardines he so often gave them.

FLEMING: Father Ignatius was certainly serious when he told the person responsible for sick members of the house that he must give them whatever food the doctor prescribed, even if various objects from the house had to be sold to pay for it.

SPANIARD: Do you remember the business of the blankets? He found out that there were only enough blankets to allow one for each person in the house. To provide any extra blankets the sick might need, he made us all draw lots to settle in what order we should give up our blankets!

Ignatius was so caring about the health of his companions because he remembered the harm he had done to himself, especially in his early pilgrim days. The disease that gave him such terrible stomach pains, and that was only finally diagnosed when he was examined after his death, was a form of gallstones. He had borne with it ever since his Paris days and would not let it interfere with his routine in Rome. In his tenth year as Father General (1550) he was so ill that he wanted to resign, but the others said, in as many words, that they would rather have a sick Ignatius as General than anyone else, however fit. He accepted their decision, and put up with the bad spells for the remaining six years (a comment of one of his doctors was that he did not take enough exercise!).

NOTES

THE 1544 JESUIT HOUSE – "dumpy rather like a shack" (see page 121). Ignatius's own rooms were somewhere high up in the house, forty-five steps from ground-level, a long way for a man with a limp. The rooms consisted of a small bedroom, a room for his Brother companion, a study, which he also used as a chapel and for receiving visitors, and a waiting-room. When the house was demolished at the end of the sixteenth century, these rooms were kept and they have survived to the present day. The rooms are at present being restored to their original appearance.

THE CHURCH OF OUR LADY OF THE WAY (see page 121) – This contained a painting of Our Lady of the Way, Ignatius's favourite one of Our Lady holding the child Jesus. The church was in a bad state of repair, which made Ignatius decide in 1549 to build a new one. However, over thirty years passed before this new one was opened. It was dedicated to the Holy Name of Jesus (in Italian it is called simply the "*Gesù*"). This is not the place to describe it, except for two especially interesting parts. At the top left-hand corner stands the grand altar of St Ignatius, beneath which his body rests: high above there is a silver statue of him in priest's vestments, with arms outstretched as though to embrace the whole world. Beside this altar is the small altar of Our Lady of the Wayside with the picture above it. The second interesting part is another highly decorated altar, that of St Francis Xavier, facing the St Ignatius altar from the far side of the church. His body does not lie beneath, for it is in Goa, but his right arm was severed, brought to Rome and placed in a case of glass and gold on this altar.

A last interesting fact is that the whole cost of building the Gesù Church was contributed by Cardinal Alexander Farnese, the nephew of Pope Paul III who was such a great friend to the companions all through their early days in Rome.

IHS. When Ignatius wanted to have a design for an official seal with which to stamp important documents, he did not choose "A.M.D.G." or "S.J.", but the old Christian abbreviation for the name of Jesus, the first three letters of which are (in Greek) IHS. Sometimes these are written, as here, in capitals, sometimes in small letters, usually with a cross worked into the H or h.

Ignatius loved to hear *church singing*, such as Solemn Mass and Vespers. In his later years when he could no longer go to these services, he would ask some fellow-Jesuit to his room to sing Alleluia's to him; when he was himself ill he liked someone to come and sing him a hymn.

15

The secret of Ignatius

Ignatius by himself

Sooner or later those who are interested in Ignatius come to wonder how it is that we know the details both of his life as a knight and courtier, and also of his experiences when he changed to become a pilgrim. Though he had his notebook, he did not, as far as we know, keep a proper diary of those years, nor did he later sit down and write about them. However hard the first companions tried, they could not persuade him to discuss them, for it did not seem at all important to him to talk about himself. But to the companions it was important, so after he had finished the Constitutions and was again seriously ill, they planned to make yet another effort.

There was not much encouragement from Ignatius even then, until by chance a Portuguese Jesuit name Goncalves arrived in Rome on business, and was given by Ignatius a job in the house which kept him in the city for two years. This priest had always wanted to meet him and ask for his advice and guidance. As they talked together one day, Ignatius decided that the best way in which he could help Goncalves solve his problems was to explain how he, Ignatius, had with God's help

solved his own problems as a young man. Goncalves had a great skill in encouraging Ignatius to
talk about himself, and after each conversation he
went off and made accurate notes of it.

For his part Ignatius, gradually seeing that the
story of his earlier life might well help other Jesuits besides Goncalves, now showed himself much
more ready to talk, in a series of interviews. Even
then, he often made difficulties saying, "I'm too
busy this month", or "Remind me every Sunday
till I have time."

Whenever an interview took place, Ignatius
would talk pacing up and down the room. He never
said, for instance, "I did this or that", but simply
used the third person, "The pilgrim started his journey..., the pilgrim spent the summer begging in
England." The story ends quite abruptly with his
arrival in Rome in 1537 with the words, "Father
Nadal knows the rest, he will tell you." Ignatius
gave his last interview in the second half of 1555:
just under a year later he died. In due course
Goncalves used his notes to make a small book.
Usually called *The Autobiography of Ignatius
Loyola*, it is short and clear and worth reading not
once but many times.

Ignatius's character

In each chapter of this book we could find a
number of things to point out about Ignatius's
character. To list and comment on them would
need at least one more complete chapter. It will be

simpler to select some of his human qualities, and then some of the special graces which God gave him in the course of his life.

He had a great gift of attracting people to himself, as well as the talent to be a leader. The latter showed up both at the time of the defence of Pamplona and later when the companions came together, for they all instinctively accepted his leadership, long before they voted for him to be Father General. Part of being a leader is enthusiasm: Ignatius possessed this in abundance and was able to fire others with his own enthusiasm.

He attracted people by what we would call "friendliness" – the real interest he showed in what they did and liked and the way they lived. As a result they felt that here was a man who understood them, whom they could rely on, to whom they could turn for help and advice (amongst his first companions, perhaps Peter Favre is the best example of this). Ignatius used his skill when he was called upon to make peace among either quarrelling citizens or quarrelling families, for once he had led each party to accept and trust him, he could then persuade them to try and respect and trust each other.

With leadership go loyalty and chivalry, two qualities which Ignatius learnt from his family and upbringing. In his days as a courtier and soldier, Ignatius's special loyalty was to his king. As a leader he experienced the loyalty of others towards himself. By chivalry he accepted the duty of his noble rank to treat all others with courtesy and thoughtfulness, always looking to help the "underdog" or to show respect for a defeated enemy – or himself accept defeat gracefully and be modest in victory.

Ignatius's courage was outstanding. It will be enough to remember how he endured the pain of the three operations on his leg, followed by the long convalescence; the many torments in later years from his stomach illnesses; the hardships of his long and dangerous journeys; the way he used to beat himself for his sins.

One would expect a man who, like Ignatius, made a fresh start in life at the age of thirty, to be in a hurry. As it was, he had a generous share of the twin virtues of patience and perseverance. He persevered in his new way of life at Manresa, in spite of the devil's temptations; with the long years of study; with his plan for starting the Jesuits in the face of all the difficulties made by the cardinals. One of his secrets was the careful way in which he planned. It was said that, whenever he made the decision to start a job, he would carry it through however long he had to wait, for the hardest part had already been done in the planning stage. In this he was a true Basque. "He has driven in the nail" was the saying, which meant that nothing would get that nail out again. We should remember that Ignatius's training as a young man in Spain was preparing him to be a leader, able to plan, take decisions and use authority: he might well have become the Governor of a Province. In fact, he had given up all such ambitions, but, even so, he was now able at the age of fifty to make use of the skills he had once for the service of the Church as founder of the Jesuits.

When speaking to Goncalves about his early

life, he said that his great desire had then been to win fame by doing the outstanding deeds he had read about in his favourite books. At the beginning of his new life he still wanted to do great deeds in imitation of Jesus, as he had read in the Gospel, and of the saints, as he had read in their lives. But what he now wanted was no longer fame. He wanted the opposite, to be forgotten, better still to be made fun of or ill-treated, as Our Lord had been so often. As he read and meditated and prayed, he knew that he was being taught to conquer himself – his pride and worldly ambition – then to find out what God wanted him to do.

In his early career his ideals could be summed up in the word "service", especially of his king. In his new career he still wanted to serve, but now it was Christ, the King of all men, whom he would serve. He imagined too, that he was offering himself to share the mission of Christ to save the whole world. Another time he imagined the three persons of God looking at the world full of sinners whom they wished to save through the second person becoming man, himself to be a servant. This was what first made Ignatius determined to go to the Holy Land to preach to the Turks. Later the Jesuits made it part of their vocation to be willing to go anywhere in the world where there might be souls to save.

Like all holy people, Ignatius had as his motive in life the love of God: he could never, so to speak, do enough for God. The well-known "A.M.D.G." – "For the greater glory of God" – was his way of expressing this. Many people, he reasoned, acted for God's glory; often there was something extra that a person could do. That "extra" – the "greater" – was what he wanted for himself and the Jesuits. Further, he had long ago seen that it is all very well for a man to say that he loves God. The real test is to find out what God wants of you and then go on to do it.

We finish this account of Ignatius's character with two sayings which are often quoted. His fellow Jesuits, when asked what he was like, would answer, "We thought of him as a giant among a lot of ordinary human beings." Someone who was not a Jesuit, but who greatly admired Ignatius, King John of Portugal, was once asked, at the time of the election of a new Pope, whom he thought the cardinals would elect. He answered, "I know whom I'd vote for if I were a cardinal – Ignatius Loyola."

The death of Ignatius

From the year in which he was elected Father General, Ignatius was constantly ill, sometimes so ill that all thought he would die. By the summer of 1556 he had been ill fifteen times, and, although this time he was worse than usual, his doctors and the companions hoped that once again he would recover. He himself, however, felt in his bones that this time he was truly dying. He was not afraid, for he had often faced death – for instance on the ramparts of Pamplona or on the high seas. Now, without any fuss about leaving his last instructions or gathering the companions together to say farewell, one evening he simply asked Polanco to go to the Pope and beg his prayers and blessing.

Polanco, thinking that he could safely leave this until the next day, joined Ignatius for supper, at which they discussed business. During the night Brother Tomasso, who was looking after Ignatius, noticed that he was restful and often uttered the words "Ay Dios!" – "My God!". In the morning he was much weaker, but seemed able to take some food, which the Brother began to prepare. Meanwhile, one of the priests came into the room, looked at Ignatius and saw that he was quietly slipping away. The others were sent for, but before they all arrived or Polanco had returned with the Pope's blessing, Ignatius Loyola was dead. It was two hours after dawn on July 31st, 1556.

The next evening they buried him in the Church of the Madonna della Strada. Later they covered the spot with a stone inscribed as follows:

IGNATIUS LOYOLA
FOUNDER AND FIRST FATHER GENERAL
OF THE SOCIETY OF JESUS
THIS STONE WAS PLACED
BY HIS COMPANIONS AND SONS

God had indeed kept his promise to be favourable to Ignatius in Rome.

Once Ignatius said there were three things which he longed for before he died. They were that the Pope would approve the Society of Jesus; that he would approve the Spiritual Exercises; that the Constitutions should be completed. All three did in fact come to pass, in the years 1540, 1548, 1551 respectively.

At Ignatius's death there were about one thousand Jesuits doing various kinds of work in such countries as Brazil, France, Germany, India, Italy, Portugal and Spain. Further, Ignatius had been making plans, in answer to the wishes of the Pope and the King of Portugal, to send some Jesuits on a mission to Ethiopia.

In our own time, over four hundred years later, Jesuits, stationed in one hundred and eleven countries, number roughly twenty-five thousand, of whom one quarter are missionaries.

16

Ignatius and the Gospel

It was whilst reading one of the "holy books", the *Life of Christ*, that Ignatius was first really attracted to the Gospel story. From the *Life of Christ* he went on to read the actual Gospels themselves.

In this chapter we have chosen the passages in the Gospels which seem to have most inspired Ignatius to plan a new way of life.

The imitation of Christ

Learn from me; for I am gentle and lowly in heart (Matthew 11:29).

Ignatius's desire was, above all, to show his love for Christ by imitating him in his own life, as exactly as possible. For example, Christ was poor, so Ignatius would be poor; because Christ travelled round Palestine preaching, Ignatius would do the same. As he grew wiser, he realized that this way of imitating Christ was not always possible but that another way would be always possible.

So the words "*Learn from me*" led Ignatius to find how Christ, in all he said and did, behaved in this "gentle and lowly" way. Then he himself strove to become "gentle and lowly".

"If any man would come after me, let him deny himself and take up his cross daily and follow me" (Luke 9:23).

By "follow me" Christ meant choosing him as a leader and living by his example. By "deny himself" Christ meant putting our own feelings and ambitions aside and conquering our pride. By "take up his cross daily" he meant being prepared to suffer for his sake because he suffered for us. In the Spiritual Exercises, Ignatius held up Christ as a leader who invites us to follow him and share his hardships, full of hope that we will also share his victory.

Teaching and preaching

Go therefore and make disciples of all nations, baptizing them in the name of the Father and of the Son and of the Holy Spirit (Matthew 28:19).

After leaving Loyola, Ignatius gradually developed the desire to help his neighbour, by preaching and teaching, to know and love God better. When his first hope – of preaching in Palestine to the Turks – was disappointed, he and his companions, once ordained, offered themselves to the Pope, leaving him to decide where to send them, but making it clear that they were ready to go anywhere, whether in Europe or overseas.

Poverty

"Take nothing for your journey, no staff, nor bag, nor bread, nor money; and do not have two tunics" (Luke 9:3).

Like the saints he had read about, Ignatius took Christ's words as meant for himself too. Hence, from Montserrat on, he was a poor man, with no fixed home and relying on begging. Here was another way of imitating Christ, who chose to be born poor and to die in poverty; who gave up his home at Nazareth; who told the apostles to live poorly when he sent them out to share his work. Ignatius regarded poverty as essential for the companions in their work, for they would be better able to travel anywhere if they had no possessions of their own and put all their trust in God.

Mockery

Herod, together with his guards, treated him with contempt and made fun of him; he put a rich cloack on him and sent him back to Pilate (Luke 23:11).

The above text and many more moved Ignatius strongly to want to share the "internal" sufferings of Christ. They are called "internal" because through them he suffered in mind, heart and feelings. Ignatius realized that at some time we all suffer – by being let down by our friends, snubbed, laughed at, unjustly accused, made to look foolish. When Ignatius was treated like this, he rejoiced to take the chance of following the example of Christ.

APPENDIX 1

The Spiritual Exercises

The *Spiritual Exercises* is a small book, consisting not of a collection of sermons or chapters on spiritual topics, but of a series of subjects about which to pray in order to find out what God wants of us. Much of the book is guidance and suggestions about prayer and the way to plan a new life (based on Ignatius's own experiences). For each subject he gives a simple scheme and usually chooses a passage from the Gospel: this he does not explain in detail, for he wants the retreat-maker to discover for himself how this part of Christ's life can help him in his own needs. At various stages Ignatius brings in a meditation of his own, e.g., on sin, on the following of Christ the King, or on the methods of Satan.

1. *The title of the book*: "Spiritual Exercises for the overcoming of self and the regulation of one's life..."

2. *A fundamental truth*: "Man has been created to praise, reverence and serve our Lord God, thereby saving his soul.

    Everything else on earth has been created for man's sake, to help him to achieve the purpose for which he has been created.

So it follows that man has to use them as far as they help and abstain from them where they hinder his purpose.

Therefore we need to train ourselves to be impartial towards all created reality..."

3 a. *Colloquy*: Ignatius suggests ending each period of prayer with a "colloquy". "The colloquy is really the kind of talk friends have with one another, or perhaps the way a servant speaks to his master, asking for some kindness or apologizing for some failure, or telling him about some matter of business and asking for his advice."

b. *Colloquy after meditation on sin*: "Let me picture Christ our Lord hanging on the cross before me, and speak to him in this way: how has he, the creator, come to be man? Knowing eternal life, how has he come to this temporal death, this death or my sins? Then, turning to myself, I will ask: What have I done for Christ? What am I doing for Christ? What must I do for Christ?"

4. *The meditation on Christ the King*: "Christ Our Lord the Eternal King, confronts the whole world: to each and all he issues his summons in these words: I am determined to bring under my control the whole world and all my enemies, and so come to the glory of my Father. To anyone, then, who chooses to join me, I offer nothing but a share in my hardships; but if he follows me in suffering he will assuredly follow me in glory."

5. *Prayer at the beginning of meditations on the life of Christ*: "I must ask for a deep-felt knowledge of Our Lord (in this scene), that I may the better love and follow him."

6. *In the meditation on Our Lord's birth* we are asked to think about "the journey they (Mary and Joseph) have to make, the hardships they have to put up with before Our Lord is born in utter destitution. After all his labours, after suffering from hunger and thirst, heat and cold, being treated with injustice and insulted, he is to die on the cross – and all for me. Thinking of this, I will derive some benefit for my soul."

7 a. *From "Two Standards" – a meditation comparing the methods of Satan and of Christ:* "Watch him (Satan) calling together countless devils, to despatch them into different cities till the whole world is covered, forgetting no province or locality, no class or single individual."

b. (*Later in the book Ignatius gives another description of Satan's methods:*) "Or again he acts like a military commander in his attempts to overcome and seize the object he has set his heart on. An officer in command of an army takes up a position, makes a reconnaissance to discover the strength... of troops in a fortified post and launches that attack at the weakest point. Similarly, the enemy of our human nature – where he finds us weakest and most defective – he attacks at that point, seeking to overthrow us."

8. *The most perfect way of serving Christ in Ignatius's eyes*: "… Granted an equal measure of praise and glory to God, I desire to be poor along with Christ in poverty rather than rich, to be insulted along with Christ so grossly insulted, rather than to be thought well of: I would rather be thought a helpless fool for the sake of Christ who was so treated, rather than to be thought wise and clever in the world's eyes."

9 a. *Prayer at the beginning of mediations on the Passion:* "The gift proper to the Passion – sorrow in company with Christ in his sorrow, being crushed with the pain that crushed Christ, tears and a deep-felt sense of suffering, because Christ suffered so much for me."
   b. *Prayer at the beginning of meditations on the Resurrection*: "… grace to be filled with joy and happiness at the thought of Christ's great glory and happiness."

10. *The last meditation in the book is entitled "Contemplation for obtaining love"*:
   (a) *"Two preliminary observations*: (i) Love should be expressed in doing rather than in protesting; (ii) Love consists in a reciprocal interchange, the lover handing over and sharing with the beloved his possessions, gifts and capacities… So, if one of them has learning, he gives it to the other who lacks it; so, too, with positions of honour or material possessions; and the other does the same."
   (b) *The petition*: "Here it will be to beg for a

deep-felt appreciation of all the blessings I have been given, that out of the fullness of my gratitude I may become completely devoted to his Divine Majesty in effective love."

APPENDIX 2

The Constitutions

The Constitutions consist of an Introduction and ten Chapters.

1. *The Introduction* contains information for an enquirer, i.e., a brief explanation of the aims of the Society and of how Jesuits live, followed by a series of questions meant to find out how suitable he is to join the Society.

Another section contains a list of "experiments" which are intended to test this suitability. Examples of the experiments are: (a) a month spent making the Spiritual Exercises, learning above all how to get to know Christ so as to choose to follow him; (b) a month spent on a pilgrimage, without money, begging from door to door, thus learning to put all one's trust in God to provide the necessities of life (we can remember the long years Ignatius lived in this way); (c) a month serving as a hospital "orderly" (as the first companions had done from their days in Venice onwards). This would help to show whether the aspiring Jesuit could put into practice Our Lord's words, "If I have washed your feet, you should wash one another's feet."

2. *Some quotations from the ten Chapters*: (The Chapters deal with such subjects as how men are

admitted into the Society; their spiritual training and studies; the Jesuit vows).

The purpose of the Society of Jesus
The aim which the Society of Jesus directly seeks is to aid its own members and their fellow-men to attain the ultimate end for which they were created.

…Our vocation is to travel through the world and to live in any part of it whatsoever where there is hope of greater service to God and of help of souls…

Spirituality
Care should be taken in general that all the members of the Society may devote themselves to the solid and perfect virtues and to spiritual pursuits, and attach greater importance to them than to learning and other natural and human gifts. For they are the interior gifts which make those exterior means effective toward the end which is sought.

The Father General
In regard to the qualities which are desirable in the Superior General, the first is that he should be closely united with God our Lord and intimate with him in prayer and all his actions…

Poverty
Poverty, as the strong wall of religious life, should be loved in its integrity as far as this is possible with God's grace… The enemy of the

human race generally tries to weaken this defence and rampart...

Obedience
...Genuine obedience considers, not the person to whom it is offered, but him for whose sake it is offered; and if it is exercised for the sake of our Creator and Lord alone, then it is the very Lord of everything who is obeyed. In no manner, therefore, ought one to consider whether he who gives the order is the cook of the house or its superior, or one person rather than another. For... obedience is not shown either to these persons or for their sake, but to God alone and only for the sake of God our Creator and Lord.

Superiors
(The following sentence occurs in a paragraph on the importance of the choice of superiors): In a general way, subjects will be what these superiors are.

Ambition
It will also be of the highest importance toward perpetuating the Society's well-being to use great diligence in precluding from it ambition, the mother of all evils in any community or congregation whatsoever. This will be accomplished by closing the door against seeking... any dignity or prelacy within the Society...

APPENDIX 3

Some letters of Ignatius

The letters of Ignatius (some six thousand have survived) were written to many kinds of people. Naturally a great number went to fellow Jesuits – individuals, groups, the whole Society; others were received by his family or by benefactors; by friends (especially those to whom he wrote to sympathize on the death of a relative); once even by the (Spanish) army in Africa. He also wrote to rulers about Jesuits who had gone to work in their countries or for whom these rulers were asking. The rulers include the Emperor Charles V, Ferdinand King of the Romans, John III of Portugal and Claude Emperor of Abyssinia. The examples we print below give just a flavour of the subjects about which he wrote.

Venice 1536: To Sister Teresa, a nun in a convent in Barcelona

[Ignatius is advising her how to deal with the methods of Satan.]

The enemy does not care whether he speaks the truth or whether he lies. His sole purpose is to overcome us. Consider attentively how the martyrs declared that they were Christ's servants when they were brought before their pagan judges. Now, when you find yourself in the presence of the enemy of human nature who is tempting you, trying to rob you of the strength which Our Lord gives you and to render you so weak and timid with his snares, won't you have the courage to say that you desire to serve Our Lord? Rather, you must answer him... that you are his follower and that you would rather die than fall away from his service.

Rome, August–September 1540: To the people of Azpeitia

[Ignatius encourages them to receive Holy Communion frequently.]

In the early Church members of both sexes received Communion daily as soon as they were old enough. But soon devotion began to cool and Communion became weekly. Then, after a considerable interval of time, as devotion became cooler still, Communion was received on only three of the principal feasts of the year, each one being left to his own choice to receive more often, either every three days or every eight days or once a month. And finally, because of our weakness and coldness, we have ended with once a year. Let it be our glory, then, out of love for so good a Lord and because of the immense benefit to our souls, to restore and renew in some way the holy practices of our forefathers – at least to the extent of monthly Confession and Communion...

Rome, early September 1541: To Fathers Salmeron and Broët

[A short extract from the instructions for these Fathers, sent by the Pope to Ireland – see pages 106.]

When we wish to win someone over and engage him in the greater service of God our Lord, we should use the same strategy for good which the enemy employs to draw a good soul to evil. He enters through the other's door and comes out his own... If men are of a lively temper, quick and merry of speech, follow their lead in your dealings with them when you talk of holy things, and do not be too serious, glum and reserved. If they are shy and retiring, slow to speak, serious... use the same manner with them, because such ways will be gratifying to them. "I became all things to all men."

Rome, 1547: To the Jesuits at the college in Coimbra (Portugal)

[The letter encourages them in various ways to aim at the highest ideals in the service of God.]

More than anything else I should wish to awaken in you the pure love of Jesus Christ, the desire for his honour and for the salvation of souls whom he has redeemed. For you are his soldiers in this Society with a special title and a special wage... His wage is everything you are and have in the natural order... His wage is also the spiritual gifts of his grace... Finally, his wage is the whole universe and everything... it contains... As though this wage were not enough, he has made himself our wage, becoming a brother in our own flesh...

Rome, 1547: To the Jesuits at the college in Padua

[They had been feeling the pinch of their poor living conditions.]

I call poverty a grace because it is a very special gift from God, as Scripture says, "Poverty and riches are from God." How much God loved it, his only-begotten Son has shown us who, coming down from the kingdom of heaven, chose to be born in poverty and to grow up in it. He loved it, not only in life, suffering hunger and thirst, without any place to lay his head, but even in death wishing to be despoiled of everything, even of water in his thirst.

[From another letter of 1552 on the same subject:]

Suppose we compare ourselves with our brothers in India, who in such corporal and spiritual toil are so ill-provided with food, in some places not even having bread, to say nothing of wine for their drink. They must get along with a bit of rice and water, or something as little nourishing. If we compare ourselves with them, I cannot think that our suffering is excessively hard.

Rome 1551: Some guidance on prayer for young Jesuits

[The young Jesuits were those engaged in study as a preparation for ordination]

Considering the end of our studies, the scholastics can hardly give themselves to prolonged meditations... they should practice the seeking of God's presence in all things, in their conversations, their walks, in all that they see, taste, hear, understand, in all their actions, since his Divine Majesty is truly in all things by his presence, power, and essence... This method is an excellent exercise to prepare us for great visitations of Our Lord, even in prayers that are rather short.

Rome 1552: To Father Nadal with a plan for defeating the Turkish fleets

[Readers will remember how the menace of the Turks at sea prevented Ignatius and the companions – and many other pilgrims – from going to the Holy Land. Here he asks Nadal for his opinion on a scheme he has thought out for defeating the Turks, and goes on to say, that if Nadal agrees, the scheme ought to be made known to the Emperor Charles V. The letter is written by Polanco for Ignatius.]

He (Ignatius) is thinking of the Turk... and the losses which the pirates are wont to inflict on the coast lands, on the souls and bodies and belongings of Christian men, (and) has come to understand in Our Lord and to hold the firm conviction that the Emperor ought to muster a great fleet and regain control of the sea... [It] can be brought about by the Emperor at a smaller expenditure than he now makes.

[A second letter on the same subject lists nine reasons in favour of the scheme, and nine more about ways of raising the money. The sources include rich religious orders, bishops, merchants, dukes and the Pope.]

Apart from what the Emperor himself could contribute from his own income... it seems that from these sources enough could be collected to maintain a large fleet... [of] more than two hundred ships... and even three hundred... If others who could do so more properly do not speak out, it might be that one of the poor members of the Society of Jesus should undertake to do so.

[It is a matter of history that, nearly twenty years

later, in 1571, Pope Pius V organized a fleet under the command of Don John of Austria, half-brother of Philip II and Charles's successor. This fleet defeated the Turks at the Battle of Lepanto.

Rome 1555: To Reginald Pole, Cardinal of England
[When Mary became Queen of England, the country returned to the Faith. Pope Julius III sent as his legate an Englishman, Cardinal Pole; Ignatius had promised the prayers of the Jesuits for the success of his mission.]

It would be impossible to explain the joy which our least Society of Jesus has felt and continues to feel... in this reconciliation of England.

[Later in the letter Ignatius speaks of the Roman and German Colleges in Rome:]

In the Roman College there are more than seventy [Jesuits]... the students of the Germanico are giving a good account of themselves... Among them is an Englishman of talent and character... and in our college an Irishman of whom we have great hopes. If your most reverend lordship could find it convenient to send a few good students to either of these colleges we hope that before long they could be sent back with great profit to their native land...

APPENDIX 4

The Spiritual Diary

What is now called *The Spiritual Journal (or Diary) of Ignatius* consists of two copy books in his own hand, written between February 1544 and February 1545. Day by day Ignatius would put down not, as in an ordinary diary, where he had been, what business he had done, whom he had met, but the thoughts and feelings about God, or that came to him from God. These might occur when he was praying alone, or saying Mass, or even in the various places where he happened to be. The passage which follows brings out his deep devotion to the Holy Trinity.

Tuesday (February 19th, 1544). On awakening in the morning... I felt much devotion with many intellectual lights and spiritual remembrances of the Most Holy Trinity, which quieted me and delighted me immensely, even to producing pressure on my chest, because of the intense love I felt for the Most Holy Trinity... and I determined to say the Mass of the Most Holy Trinity. On the way to Mass and just before it, I was not without tears; an abundance of them during it, but very peacefully, with very many lights and spiritual memories concerning the Most Holy Trinity which served as a great illumination to my mind, so much so, that I thought I could never learn so much by hard study, and later... I felt and understood, I thought, more than if I had studied all my life.

MAN OF THE BEATITUDES

Pier Giorgio Frassati

by Luciana Frassati

"The man of the eight beatitudes" – this is how John Paul II described Pier Giorgio Frassati, otherwise known to his friends as "Robespierre" or "The Terrible". Born in Turin in 1901, the only son of Alfredo Frassati – founder of the prestigious Italian newspaper, *La Stampa* – Pier Giorgio "represented the pure, happy, fine Christian youth interested in social problems, who had the Church and its fate at heart" (Karl Rahner). A magnificent athlete and gifted with exuberant high spirits and humour, Pier Giorgio bore a courageous witness of Christian faith and charity to others, especially towards the very poor and suffering. A fatal illness cut short Pier Giorgio's life at the premature age of 24. Young men and women will find in Pier Giorgio an inspiring Christian model in facing the challenges of modern times.

LUCIANA FRASSATI, Pier Giorgio's sister, was born in 1902 in Pollone, Italy. She graduated with honours in jurisprudence in 1923. Married to a Polish diplomat, and the mother of six children, she devoted much time and her literary skill in publishing books about the life and personality of her brother Pier Giorgio.

ISBN 085439 286 6   187 pages   £5.95

NOT PEACE BUT A SWORD

John Henry Newman

by Felicity O'Brien

'He followed the truth wherever it led him'. This description by Cardinal Newman of someone who greatly influenced him in his early life may be applied to Newman himself. At the age of 15 he underwent a conversion experience. From then on he pursued the truth 'wherever it led him'. The autor, delving into a large collection of letters, sermons, articles and books by Newman, portrays him as a passionate seeker of holiness and a champion of truth. In times when indifference can masquerade as tolerance, and steadfast loyalty to a creed can degenerate into religious fanaticism, this book cuts finely through the mists of both apathy and bigotry, and offers to the reader the companionship of an unshakable believer.

FELICITY O'BRIEN is a freelance writer. For a number of years she worked with the Catholic weekly, The Universe. *From there she moved on to take charge of the publications department of the Independent Broadcasting Authority. She lives in Kent.*

ISBN 085439 327 7   185 pages   £5.95

THROUGH THE EYE OF A NEEDLE
Frédéric Ozanam

by Austin Fagan

Child of the 19th century, Frédéric Ozanam is an extraordinarily relevant figure for our time.

Exceptionally gifted with a precocious intelligence and a prophetic intuition, he had at a very early age, the foreboding of the tearings of our world and the cleavage between the strong and the weak, the rich and the poor.

Dr Austin Fagan has accurately described the various aspects of the rich personality of the principal founder of the Society of St Vincent de Paul: delicacy of family feelings, sense of friendship, spiritual radiance, professional conscientiousness, dedication to public affairs. Frédéric's was a truly prophetic voice that can still inspire many to speak out and act with the poor and the underprivileged of society today.

*DR AUSTIN FAGAN, a graduate of Manchester University, was awarded a M Litt for his thesis entitled*The political and social ideas of Antoine-Frédéric Ozanam (1813-53) and their relationship to the movement of ideas in his time. *In 1988 he was elected President of Manchester SVP Central Council and also became a Vice-President of the National Council.*

ISBN 085439 313 7   212 pages   £5.95

NO GREATER LOVE

Damien apostle of the lepers

by John Milsome

This is the story of a man – Joseph de Veuster, better known as Father Damien, "the hero of Molokai" – who devoted his life to the welfare of the lepers on the island of Molokai, in the Pacific Ocean. The conditions on the island were daunting. The lepers lived in squalor and misery. Being a foreigner he was not at once welcomed by the lepers. His "ragged honesty, generosity and mirth" however, won them over as friends. What is Damien's relevance for us today? Basically three things: fidelity to one's calling, dedication to a worthy cause and compassion for the underprivileged and outcasts of the society.

Robert Louis Stevenson wrote of Damien: "It was his part, by one striking act of martyrdom, to direct all men's eyes on this distressful country. At a blow and with the price of his life, he made the place illustrious and public... If ever any man brought reforms and died to bring them, it was he." This is the challenge unfolded in the pages of *No Greater Love*.

JOHN MILSOME was born in Pinner, Middlesex. He trained as a teacher and his main interest outside teaching was his writing career. The completion of No Greater Love *was sealed with his premature death.*

ISBN 085439 308 0   105 pages   £5.25

THE CHEERFUL GIVER
Margaret Sinclair

by Felicity O'Brien

Margaret Ann Sinclair was born on 29th March 1900, in Edinburgh. For twenty-three years she lived an ordinary family life reaching out to people with her constant serenity and cheerfulness. She joined the Poor Clares in 1923, and died of tuberculosis at the age of twenty-five.

Margaret's holiness was already manifest among her contemporaries. She is an outstanding example and source of inspiration for Christians today.

FELICITY O'BRIEN is a freelance writer. For a number of years she worked with the Catholic weekly, The Universe. *From there she moved on to take charge of the publications department of the Independent Broadcasting Authority. She lives in Kent.*

ISBN 085439 310 2   89 pages   £4.25